D1535704

Instructor's Manual
to Accompany

SOFTWARE
ENGINEERING

A PRACTITIONER'S APPROACH

THIRD EDITION

ROGER S. PRESSMAN, Ph.D.

McGraw-Hill, Inc.
New York St. Louis San Francisco Auckland Bogotá
Caracas Lisbon London Madrid Mexico Milan
Montreal New Delhi Paris San Juan Singapore
Sydney Tokyo Toronto

Instructor's Manual to Accompany
SOFTWARE ENGINEERING
A PRACTITIONER'S APPROACH
Third Edition
Copyright©1992 by McGraw-Hill, Inc. All rights reserved.
Printed in the United States of America. The contents, or
parts thereof, may be reproduced for use with

SOFTWARE ENGINEERING
A PRACTITIONER'S APPROACH
Third Edition
by Roger S. Pressman

ISBN 0-07-050815-1

    4 5 6 7 8 9 0 HAM HAM 9 0 9 8 7 6 5

TABLE OF CONTENTS

PREFACE

Few people involved with computers in academia, industry or government would question the importance of software in the computer-based systems of the 1990s. As software technology advances, we need methods for a controlled, systematic approach to software development. Software engineering—a field that combines principles of project management, computer science and engineering methodology—is an essential element of software development. It is a topic that should be studied by all industry practitioners and taught in all serious computer science and computer engineering programs.

Prior to the first edition of *Software Engineering: A Practitioner's Approach* (SEPA), there were no textbooks that adequately treated the entire software engineering process, while at the same time presenting the subject in a style that is amenable to a University or industrial course format. There were fewer than 10 institutions in the United States that offered a software engineering course. In the decade that has passed since that time, software engineering courses (of one type or another) are now offered at over 400 institutions in the US and in hundreds of Universities worldwide. Many books on the subject are now published.

The third edition of *Software Engineering: A Practitioner's Approach* (SEPA) represents my best attempt at providing a reasonably comprehensive guide for software engineering. A review of the second edition in *IEEE Software* (January, 1988) called the second edition "a software engineer's Baedecker's Guide." I thought this really did capture the essence of the book. My intent in each of the editions has been to provide a travel guide for engineering students and practitioners as they begin their journey into this important technology.

A travel guide cannot provide street maps of every town or list every phone number of every inhabitant of a country. Similarly, a software engineering travel guide cannot present comprehensive coverage of every important topic or it will become prohibitively long (after all, this third edition numbers well over

750 pages!). Both can, however, select those things that the author believes are important and teach you enough about the language, the main routes, the customs, the laws and the taboos to enable you to make your journey a pleasant one. If you intend to be a native, more detailed study, conducted over many years, will be necessary.

I have been overwhelmed by the widespread acceptance and use of the first and second editions of SEPA—over 100,000 copies have been sold worldwide. In writing the third edition, I have attempted to extend both the breadth and depth of earlier editions, while at the same time maintaining the attributes that have lead to the book's success. With the publication of this edition, I have also assembled the *Software Engineering Teaching System* (see segment 2 of this Instructor's Manual). I hope it provides you with assistance in your teaching.

During my years as a professor at the University of Bridgeport, I had an opportunity to review many instructor's manuals. My goal for this one has been to develop the kind of supplementary tool that I have often desired, but rarely encountered. I hope that you find this manual useful.

Roger S. Pressman
Orange, Connecticut
June, 1991

ACKNOWLEDGEMENTS

The third edition of *Software Engineering: A Practitioner's Approach* and the resultant content of this *Instructor's Manual* have been influenced by the comments and suggestions of colleagues and students too numerous to mention. A student's question, a colleague's request for additional information, or a Professor's suggestion (some from as far away as Japan and Australia) have each in their own way contributed to the content of both the book and this manual. My thanks to all of you.

I am also indebted to all of the industry vendors who have agreed to participate in the creation of the *Software Engineering Teaching System*. Their generosity and ready willingness to help in some small way to improve the quality of software engineering instruction have been quite edifying.

In addition, my sincere appreciation to Elaine Kant for allowing me to use her paper as a foundation for Segment 5 of this manual. Her work remains one of the best "how to" guides for conducting a software engineering course.

Special thanks go to Dave Levine, my bionic associate, who has helped in many ways large and small as the book and the manual have come together.

Writing an instructor's manual comes as a shock to most authors. You've just finished one book and you have to write another one under significant time pressure. My family—Barbara, Mathew and Michael—understands the challenges and allows me to meet them. For that, my love and thanks.

FORETHOUGHT

A great teacher is my adversary, my conqueror, commissioned to chastise me. He leaves me tame and grateful for the new language he has purloined from other kings whose granaries are filled and whose libraries are famous. He tells me that teaching is the art of theft: of knowing what to steal and from whom.

Bad teachers do not touch me; the great ones never leave me. They ride with me during all my days, and I pass on to others what they have imparted to me. I exchange their handy gifts with strangers on trains, and I pretend the gifts are mine. I steal from the great teachers. And the truly wonderful thing about them is they would applaud my theft, laugh at the thought of it, realizing they had taught me their larcenous skills well.

Patrick Conroy
The Lords of Discipline
Houghton Mifflin Co., 1980.

1 INTRODUCTION TO SEPA

Software Engineering: A Practitioner's Approach (abbreviated SEPA in this guide) provides a foundation for university and industry courses in software engineering. The book presents the entire software engineering process—definition, development, and maintenance—in a partitioned fashion that is amenable to term (quarter, trimester, or semester) courses at the University level. SEPA can also be used with success as the text for industry training courses ("short courses") in software engineering.

The topic that we call software engineering is both exciting and frustrating. Exciting because it draws on many technical disciplines and provides a harness that binds each discipline to the next. Frustrating, because it demands knowledge in a multitude of topic areas and seems to be infinitely expandable. SEPA does not purport to be *the* definitive volume on software engineering—no text can satisfy such a goal because the field is changing too rapidly. Rather, this book does present a thorough treatment of software engineering, allowing the instructor to emphasize and augment (with state-of-the-art material) those subjects that are relevant to course participants.

This third edition of SEPA is accompanied by a *Software Engineering Teaching System* that has been organized to provide you with a wide variety of teaching options. Ten video tape modules on various software engineering topics, over 200 transparencies for classroom use, and real (not toy) industry quality CASE tools are available to you to help in teaching this important subject.

This *Instructor's Manual* has been written to assist you in the development and presentation of a course in software engineering. The manual includes a description of teaching options, guidelines for the use of the *Software Engineering Teaching System,*course design considerations and a chapter-by-chapter discussion of the book.

1.1 OVERVIEW OF THE BOOK

The twenty-four chapters of the third edition have been divided into five parts. This has been done to compartmentalize topics and assist instructors who may not have the time or inclination to complete the entire book in one term. Different parts of the book can be used in conjunction with other elements of the *Software Engineering Teaching System* (described in detail in segment 2 of this manual) and will enable you to create lecture or lab courses that emphasize those topics that are relevant to your curriculum.[1]

Part I—*Software, the Process and Its Management*—presents a thorough treatment of software project management issues. It can be used in conjunction with portions of Parts IV and V if you intend to teach the course with a project management emphasis.

Part II—*Software and System Requirements Analysis*—contains five chapters that cover analysis fundamentals and requirements modeling methods and notation. It can be used alone or in conjunction with Parts III and IV, if your primary emphasis is technical methods for software development.

Part III—*The Design and Implementation of Software*—presents a thorough treatment of software design, emphasizing fundamental design criteria that lead to high quality systems and design methods that translate an analysis model into a software solution. It can be used as the core of a design course or in conjunction with Parts III, IV, and V, if your primary emphasis is design but you want to provide broader coverage.

Part IV—*Ensuring, Verifying and Maintaining System Integrity*—emphasizes the activities that are applied to ensure quality throughout the software engineering process. Although I do not recommend using this part as the core of a course, it complements other parts of SEPA as indicated above.

Part V—*The Role of Automation*—discusses the impact of CASE on the software development process. Used in conjunction with Parts I, II, III and/or IV, this part of SEPA introduced students to one of the hottest topics in software engineering.

---

[1] SEPA 3/e conforms well to the new draft *ACM/IEEE Computing Curriculum 1991* and accommodates the "knowledge unit" concept well. This will be discussed in segment 3 of this Manual.

In summary, the five part organization of the third edition enables you to "cluster" topics based on available time and student need. An entire one term course can be build around one or more of the five parts. By organizing the third edition in this way, I have attempted to provide you with a number of teaching options, while providing your students with a software engineering textbook that introduces them to the broad scope of the subject and can serve them as a reference in future years.

A more detailed discussion of each SEPA chapter is presented in segment 5 of this manual.

1.2 DIFFERENCES BETWEEN THE SECOND AND THIRD EDITIONS

The third edition of *Software Engineering: A Practitioner's Approach* [Note: To make the distinction between editions, I'll use the designation SEPA 2 and SEPA 3 for this section only] is considerably more than a minor rewrite and update of the second edition. The third edition contains expanded discussion of nearly every topic presented in SEPA 2 and introduces many, many topics that were not even mentioned in the second edition. SEPA 3 has been partitioned into five parts to facilitate course design and has been augmented by the *Software Engineering Teaching System*. Many new **Problems and Points to Ponder** have been added. The **Further Readings** sections have been revised and many new figures and examples are used.The following table identifies key changes on a chapter by chapter basis.

TABLE OF CHANGES FOR SEPA, THIRD EDITION

<u>Chapter</u>	<u>3rd edition revisions</u>
1	Updates and extends SEPA 2, Chapter 1. The concept of the "aging software plant is introduced, new paradigms are discussed.
2	*New chapter*. Extracts some information from SEPA 2, Chapter 3, but introduces much new information on management metrics. Also includes increased emphasis on function point metric.

TABLE OF CHANGES FOR SEPA, THIRD EDITION (continued)

Chapter	3rd edition revisions
3	*New chapter.* Extracts liberally from the first part of SEPA 2, Chapter 3. Deletes some dated estimation models and introduces new ones.
4	*New chapter.* Extracts from the second part of SEPA 2, Chapter 3. Introduces major new section on risk analysis.
5.	Updates and extends SEPA, Chapter 2. New emphasis on system modeling; new discussion of system simulation.
6.	Updates and extends SEPA 2, Chapter 4. Additional discussion of FAST techniques and minor revisions/update throughout.
7	*New chapter.* Extracts from the first part of SEPA 2, Chapter 5 and a small portion of SEPA 2, Chapter 10. Presents structured analysis approach for both conventional and real-time systems. New examples.
8	*New chapter.* All new presentation of object-oriented concepts and OOA notation.
9	*New chapter.* Extracts from the second part of SEPA 2, Chapter 5 and adds all new sections on formal specification methods, including detailed example. JSD and DSSD have been de-emphasized in this edition.
10	Updates SEPA 2, Chapter 6.
11	Updates SEPA 2, Chapter 7. New example throughout.
12	Major update of SEPA 2, Chapter 9. Introduces new notation and examples.

TABLE OF CHANGES FOR SEPA, THIRD EDITION (continued)

Chapter	3rd edition revisions
13	Updates SEPA 2, Chapter 8.
14	*New chapter.* All new presentation of interface design.
15	Major update of SEPA 2, Chapter 10. New sections on simulation tools and techniques.
16	Updates SEPA 2, Chapter 11.
17	Major update of SEPA 2, Chapter 12. New sections on statistical SQA, software reliability, software quality metrics, and software safety. Revised discussion of formal technical reviews.
18	Updates SEPA 2, Chapter 13. New discussion of condition and data flow testing.
19	Updates SEPA 2, Chapter 14.
20	*New chapter.* Extracts from the first part of SEPA 2, Chapter 15 and a small part of SEPA 2, Chapter 8. New sections on reverse and re-engineering.
21	*New chapter.* Extracts from the second part of SEPA 2, Chapter 15. Major new sections of configuration objects, SCM tasks.
22	*New chapter.* All new presentation on CASE tools.
23	*New chapter.* All new presentation on I-CASE and software development environments, the repository, and integration issues.
24	*New chapter.* All new presentation that discusses the future direction of software engineering.

1.3 AUDIENCES FOR THE BOOK

SEPA may be used as a textbook for a course in software engineering for the following audiences:

1. *Undergraduate students* in computer science, engineering and (possibly) management/information science. Students are expected to have a nontrivial (i.e., considerably more than an introductory programming course) background in software and would generally be at Junior/Senior level. Guidelines for courses for this audience are presented in segment 4.

2. *Graduate students* in computer science, engineering and other related disciplines. A course for this audience may be tailored to the technical maturity and backgrounds of the students. Alternative modes of presentation are also discussed in segment 4.

3. *Practicing professionals* from commercial, engineering, scientific and systems environments. A course for this audience (generally an intensive 3 to 5 day format) must be tailored to the technical background and interests of the participants. Alternative modes of presentation are discussed in segment 5.

1.4 TEACHING OPTIONS

Because software engineering is such a broad subject, the instructor of a course may present a balanced treatment of all topics or may choose to emphasize one or more areas. Your background and the needs of your students will dictate this choice.

At the undergraduate computer science and engineering level, greater emphasis may be placed on development issues (analysis, design, coding, testing). For undergraduate courses directed toward M.I.S. backgrounds, emphasis may shift to project management, specification, QA, and maintenance. Similar choices can be made for graduate courses.

In an academic setting, a software engineering course can be offered as:

1. a lecture, problem, test course;

2. a lecture, project course;
3. a project course (with readings from SEPA);
4. some combination of choices 1 – 3.

For maximum, pedagogical benefit, a project is generally recommended. Segments 3 and 4 discusses options for course design.

In a continuing education/professional training setting, a software engineering course can be offered as:

1. a lecture, "laboratory" course;
2. a seminar or tutorial;
3. a lecture-project course.

Segment 5 discusses options for course design in this area.

A note of caution: You should resist the temptation to offer a classical "advanced programming course" that is called "Software Engineering." Software engineering is much more than advanced programming and unless your course has been explicitly design to emphasize only one topic area, the course offering should clearly present topics relevant to each phase in the software engineering process. Emphasis may vary, but a presentation that is limited to "algorithm design, data design, structured programming and debugging" (however worthwhile as an independent course offering) is not an adequate presentation of software engineering.

1.5 USE OF THIS MANUAL

The *Instructor's Manual* for SEPA has been written to provide you with guidelines for course design, a description of the *Software Engineering Teaching System* courseware that you can use to complement SEPA, and an explanation of chapter content, problems and points to ponder, and supplementary references and topics.

Segment 2 describes *Software Engineering Teaching System* courseware and provides you with instructions on how to get it. Segment 3 discusses the new *IEEE/ACM Computing Curriculum 1991* and how SEPA can be used to fulfill many of the "knowledge units" described in the draft curriculum. Segment 4 provides detailed information for the design of a university level course. Segment 5 provides guidelines for those instructors who are contemplating the development of a software engineering short-course or seminar. Segment 6 provides valuable insight into the content of each chapter and serves as a support tool for those who have adopted SEPA. Appendix I contains an extensive software engineering bibliography that you may find useful in lecture preparation, research and student assignments. Appendix II contains additional information and ordering information for the *Software Engineering Teaching System*.

2 SOFTWARE ENGINEERING TEACHING SYSTEM

I've had a fair amount of experience in teaching software engineering and there are a few things I've learned along the way:

• Software engineering courses are not amenable to chalk board presentations—too much time is wasted with no benefit.
• No instructor is expert in all subject areas and another point of view freshens the course.
• Modern software engineering is a tools-based technology—teaching the subject without reference to and demonstration of CASE tools is often sterile.

With these thoughts in mind, I decided to develop courseware to supplement the third edition of SEPA. When I began, my intention was to do little more than I had done for the second edition—an instructor's manual and some transparencies. The final result, I hope you'll agree, is substantially more than that.

To be honest, my thoughts while assembling a more comprehensive set of courseware for the third edition of SEPA were not completely altruistic. There are dozens of software engineering books on the market (some good, some not so good) and it's important to consider ways to differentiate an offering. I'm convinced that depth of coverage, style and overall presentation differentiate SEPA in its own right (but it's hard to be objective). However, I honestly do believe that my attempt to provide supplementary courseware—the *Software Engineering Teaching System*—makes SEPA unique among all textbooks on the subject.

2.1 THE SOFTWARE ENGINEERING TEACHING SYSTEM

The *Software Engineering Teaching System* includes the third edition of *Software Engineering: A Practitioner's Approach*, this *Instructor's Manual*, a collection of industry quality CASE tools, ten video-tape modules that introduce important concepts in software engineering and CASE, workbooks to go along with the video tapes (if you decide to assign the tape outside the classroom), and a complete set of transparencies to complement your lectures.

To put together the teaching system, I decided to use only industry quality products. Real CASE tools, not toys. Real video that is for sale worldwide, not lectures taped with a camcorder fixed in the back of a classroom. Transparencies that are used for industry training, not thrown together using the artwork from the textbook as the exclusive source. The problem with this strategy is that industry quality products are often beyond the reach of many department budgets. So I began to negotiate. Digital Equipment Corporation graciously agreed to provide the video series for a reproduction charge only. A number of CASE vendors enthusiastically agreed to provide their products at a deep discount that covers only their cost of fulfilment. R.S. Pressman & Associates, Inc. (the president of the company had substantial influence!) agreed to provide transparencies that the company uses for industry training.

2.2 TRANSPARENCIES

Over 200 hundred transparencies are provided to complement your lectures. They are organized on a chapter-by chapter basis and have been designed both to emphasize important topics presented in each SEPA chapter and (in some cases) to introduce additional topics for discussion. The transparencies are available from McGraw-Hill at no cost to all colleges and universities that have adopted SEPA.[1]

2.3 VIDEO MODULES

The video portion of the *Software Engineering Teaching System* is entitled "Understanding CASE" and has been developed in conjunction with Digital Equipment Corporation. The series is a set of 10 video modules and workbooks organized in three parts:

---

[1] A request form for the transparencies may be found at the back of this manual. Please note the terms and conditions for their use.

Part I—Management Issues and Strategies
Module 1. Challenges of Software Development
Module 2. CASE: A Technology Overview
Module 3. Making Software Engineering Happen

Part II—Software Quality and Configuration Management
Module 4. Software Configuration Management
Module 5. Software Quality Assurance
Module 6. Software Testing
Module 7. Software Maintenance and CASE

Part III—Analysis, Design and CASE Technical Issues
Module 8. Software Requirements Analysis and Specification
Module 9. Software Design
Module 10. CASE: Technical Issues

Each video module is approximately one hour in length and is supplemented with a workbook that contains figures, further points of discussion and suggested references.

The video portion of the *Software Engineering Teaching System* can be used in two different ways:

• as an alternative to one or more of your lectures (the modules are approximately 50 – 60 minutes in length, making them idea for the standard classroom period
• as an outside learning resource

Both approaches have merits and in some cases can be used in combination. You may choose to use a few modules during lecture time and in addition place the entire series in your library's media center (where it can be effectively controlled). Video modules can then be assigned for (mandatory or optional) outside viewing.

One set of the video series may be obtained by any college or university that has adopted SEPA for classroom use. Requests for the video series should be sent directly to the McGraw-Hill Book Company using the special request form contained in Appendix II of this *Instructors Manual*. The terms and conditions that apply to the use of these video modules are described in the appendix.

2.4 CASE TOOLS

Modern software engineering is conducted using CASE tools. It should be taught in a way that allows student to experience the tools and understand their strengths and weaknesses. Some computer science and computer engineering department have CASE tools labs that are equipped with a variety of high caliber tool, but many do note. It is for this reason that the *Software Engineering Teaching System* has CASE tools as an important component.

CASE tools are available to help you teach the basics of project planning and software analysis and design.

Appendix II contains reproductions of vendor supplied literature that describes each of the CASE tools that are available as part of the *Software Engineering Teaching System*. Please read the tool description carefully to be sure that you have a hardware environment that can support the tool.

One tool, selected from each of the categories noted above, may be obtained by any college or university that has adopted SEPA for classroom use. Requests for individual CASE tools should be sent directly to the CASE tools vendor, *but only after you have received a validated order card from McGraw-Hill*. Details for ordering are presented in Appendix II of this *Instructor's Manual*. The terms and conditions that apply to the use of these video modules are also described in the appendix.

3 SEPA AND THE ACM/IEEE COMPUTING CURRICULUM

At the time of this writing, the ACM/IEEE-CS Joint Curriculum Task Force is finalizing *Computing Curricula—1991*. The executive summary of a draft of the this lengthy report introduces the curricula in the following manner:[1]

> This report contains curricular recommendations for baccalaureate programs in the discipline of computer science and computer engineering, known simply as computing. These recommendations provide a uniform basis for curriculum design across all segments of the educational community—schools and colleges of engineering, arts and sciences, and liberal arts. This report is the first comprehensive undergraduate curriculum report to be endorsed by both of the major professional societies in the computing discipline—the Association for Computing Machinery and the Computer Society of the IEEE ... .
>
> The organization of subject mater in this report follows that presented in the 1988 report *Computing as a Discipline*. The subject matter is drawn from nine fundamental areas:
>
> > Algorithms and Data Structures
> > Architecture
> > Artificial Intelligence and Robotics
> > Database and Information Retrieval
> > Human-Computer Communication
> > Numerical and Symbolic Computation
> > Operating Systems
> > Programming Languages
> > Software Methodology and Engineering
>
> The common requirements do not appear here as a single group of courses. Rather, they appear as smaller packages of closely related topics known as *knowledge units*. Different institutions will combine these knowledge units into courses in different ways to meet their particular needs and priorities....

---

[1]   Note that all extracts were obtained from the *draft* report dated 14 November 90. The final version may vary somewhat, but it is unlikely that major changes will be made.

These recommendations also recognize that mastery of the discipline includes not only an understanding of basic subject matter, but also an understanding of the three processes, or "points of view," that computing professionals employ and students need to appreciate: theory, abstraction, and design. Undergraduate programs should ensure that students master each of these three processes. Particular attention is paid, to the importance of laboratory work as it reinforces student mastery of concepts and their application to real-world problems.

The third edition of SEPA has been designed to assist you in presenting theory, abstraction and design as it relates to "software methodology and engineering." In the sections that follow, an overview of all common requirements noted in *Computing Curricula—1991* to help you understand where the ACM/IEEE-CS joint tasks views software engineering in context. Then the knowledge units associated with software engineering are presented in more detail.

3.1 SUMMARY OF COMMON REQUIREMENTS FROM COMPUTING CURRICULUM—1991

A complete list of the titles of the knowledge units that comprise the common requirements for *Computing Curricula—1991* are listed below. The recommended number of lecture hours associated with each fundamental area is noted in parentheses.

AL: Algorithms and data structures (approx. 47 lecture hours)
    AL1: Basic Data Structures
    AL2: Abstract Data Types
    AL3: Recursive Algorithms
    AL4: Complexity Analysis
    AL5: Complexity Classes
    AL6: Sorting and Searching
    AL7: Computability and Undecidability
    AL8: Problem-Solving Strategies
    AL9: Parallel and Distributed Algorithms

AR: Architecture (approx. 59 lecture hours)
    AR1: Digital Logic
    AR2: Digital Systems
    AR3: Machine Level Representation of Data
    AR4: Assembly Level Machine Organization
    AR5: Memory System Organization and Architecture
    AR6: Interfacing and Communication

AR7: Alternative Architectures

AI: Artificial Intelligence and Robotics (approx. 9 lecture hours)
    AI1: History and Applications of Artificial Intelligence
    AI2: Problems, State Spaces, and Search Strategies

DB: Database and Information Retrieval (approx. 9 lecture hours)
    DB1: Overview, Models, and Applications of Database Systems
    DB2: The relational Data Model

HU: Human-Computer Communication (approx. 8 lecture hours)
    HU1: User Interfaces
    HU2: Computer Graphics

NU: Numerical and Symbolic Computation (approx. 7 lecture hours)
    NU1: Number Representation, Errors, and Portability
    NU2: Iterative Approximation Methods

OS: Operating Systems (approx. 31 lecture hours)
    OS1: History, Evolution, and Philosophy
    OS2: Tasking and Processes
    OS3: Process Coordination and Synchronization
    OS4: Scheduling and Dispatch
    OS5: Physical and Virtual Memory Organization
    OS6: Device Management
    OS7: File Systems and Naming
    OS8: Security and Protection
    OS9: Communications and Networking
    OS10: Distributed and Real-time Systems

PL: Programming Language (approx. 46 lecture hours)
    PL1: History and Overview of Programming Languages
    PL2: Virtual Machines
    PL3: Representation of Data Types
    PL4: Sequence Control
    PL5: Data Control, Sharing, and Type Checking
    PL6: Run-time Storage Management
    PL7: Finite State Automata and Regular Expressions
    PL8: Context-Free Grammars and Pushdown Automata
    PL8: Language Translation Systems
    PL10: Programming Language Semantics
    PL11: Programming Paradigms
    PL12: Distributed and Parallel Programming Constructs

SE: Software Methodology and Engineering (approx. 44 lecture hours)
SE1: Fundamental Problem-solving Concepts
SE2: The Software Development Process
SE3: Software Requirements and Specifications
SE4: Software Design and Implementation
SE5: Verification and Validation

SP: Social, Ethical, and Professional Issues (approx. 11 lecture hours)
SP1: Historical and Social Context of Computing
SP2: Responsibilities of the Computing Professional
SP3: Risks and Liabilities
SP4: Intellectual Property

The topics in the following list should be considered as areas where courses may be developed to provide in-depth study in advanced undergraduate and graduate courses. Other topics beyond these are important as well, but will vary with the particular interests and expertise of the faculty in individual programs. However, the topics below tend to be so significant to the discipline at this time that several of them ought to appear among the advanced courses offered by any undergraduate program.

Advanced Operating Systems
Advanced Software Engineering
Analysis of Algorithms
Artificial Intelligence
Combinational and Graph Algorithms
Computational Complexity
Computer Communication Networks
Computer Graphics
Computer-Human Interface
Computer Security
Data base and Information Retrieval
Digital Design Automation
Fault-Tolerant Computing
Information Theory
Modeling and Simulation
Numerical Computation
Parallel and Distributed Computing
Performance Prediction and Analysis
Principles of Computer Architecture
Principles of Programming Languages
Programming Language Translation
Real-Time Systems
Robotics and Machine Intelligence
Semantics and Verification
Societal Impact of Computing
Symbolic Computation
Theory of Computation
VLSI System Design

3.2 CURRICULUM REQUIREMENTS FOR SOFTWARE ENGINEERING AND METHODOLOGY

The *Computing Curriculum—1991* recommendations for software engineering divide the topic into five knowledge units that are described in this section. After the descriptions, I have attempted to indicate how SEPA addresses the topics noted. The information presented in this section should be used in conjunction with the course design information presented in segment 4 of this Instructor's Manual.

The ACM/IEEE-CS report describes software methodology and engineering in the following manner:

There are approximately 44 hours of lectures recommended for this set of knowledge units.

The knowledge units in the common requirements for the subject area of Software Methodology and Engineering emphasize the following topics: fundamental problem solving concepts, the software development process, software specifications, software design and implementation, verification, and validation.

SE1: Fundamental Problem-Solving Concepts

Introduction to the basic ideas of algorithmic problem solving and programming, using principles of top-down design, stepwise refinement, and procedural abstraction. Basic control structure, data types, and input/output conventions.

Recurring Concepts: conceptual and formal models, consistency and completeness, levels of abstraction.

Lecture Topics: (16 hours minimum)

1. Procedural abstraction; parameters
2. Control structures: selection, iteration, recursion
3. Data types; e.g., numbers, strings, booleans, and their uses in problem solving
4. The software design process; from specification to implementation; stepwise refinement; graphical representation

Suggested Laboratories:

1. (closed) Exercise a given program that solves a simple prespecified problem. Trace the values of selected variables and answer specific questions about the program's behavior. Students will become familiar with the elements of program behavior, and the correspondence between the steps of its execution and the problem that it solves.
2. (open) Design a program that solves a simple prespecified problem.
3. (open) Design procedures that realize that individual steps reflected in the pseudocode solution to a more intricate problem. Each procedure should be documented by way of precise specifications, and implemented with appropriate parameters.
4. (closed) Implement a search problem, first using iteration and then using recursion. Trace the execution of both implementations, and contrast their run-time characteristics. Determine which is best, and under what circumstances.
5. (open) Design and implement a simple sorting program (e.g., insertion or bubble sort), and demonstrate that it meets the specifications of sorting.

Connections:

Related to : PR ^{2}
Prerequisites:
Requisite for: AL1, AL2, AL3, AR2, DB2, HU2, NU2, PL3, SE3,

The topics suggested for **SE1** are covered in detail in Part III of SEPA. The majority of information can be obtained from Chapter 10, with additional information presented in Chapters 6 and 12.

SE2: The Software Development Process

Introduction to models and issues concerned with the development of high quality software. Use of tools and environments that facilitate the design and implementation of large software systems. The role and use of standards.

Recurring Concepts: complexity of large problems, conceptual and formal models, consistency and completeness.

Lecture Topics: (eight hours minimum)

1. Software life-cycle models; e.g., waterfalls, prototyping, and iterative development
2. Software design objectives
3. Documentation

---

^{2} SE1 can either follow PR or be intermixed with it.

4. Configuration management and control
5. Software reliability issues: safety, responsibility, risk assessment
6. Maintenance
7. Specification and design tools, implementation tools

Suggested Laboratories:

1. (open) Implement a prototype for a given specification.
2. Given a software design and an intermediate implementation in an iterative development, complete the next iterative implementation.
3. Criticize a given set of documentation for a software product.
4. Given the code and specifications for a software implementation, along with a modified set of specifications, modify the code to conform to the new specifications. Describe documentation that would have been useful in performing the modification.

Connections:
> Related to : SP3. SE3
> Prerequisites: SE1, AL2
> Requisite for: SE4

The topics suggested for **SE2** are covered in detail throughout SEPA. Relevant SEPA chapters are noted in parentheses following the list of lecture topics:
1. Software life-cycle models; e.g., waterfalls, prototyping, and iterative development (SEPA Chapter 1)
2. Software design objectives (SEPA Chapter 10)
3. Documentation (see SEPA index under *Documentation*)
4. Configuration management / control (SEPA Chapter 21)
5. Software reliability issues: safety, responsibility, risk assessment (SEPA Chapter 17)
6. Maintenance (SEPA Chapter 20)
7. Specification and design tools, implementation tools (SEPA Chapter 22, 23)

In my opinion, the number of lecture hours recommended (8 hours minimum) is inadequate to cover the material noted. I believe that between 12 hours (minimum) and 18 hours are necessary to adequately convey important concepts.

SE3: Software Requirements and Specifications

Introduction to the development of formal and informal specifications for defining software system requirements.

Recurring Concepts: Complexity of large problems, conceptual and formal models, levels of abstraction, reuse.

Lecture Topics: (four hours minimum)

1. Informal specifications
2. Formal specifications: preconditions and postconditions, algebraic specifications for ADT's

Suggested Laboratories:

1. Given an informal problem statement, or a user group with an implementation request, perform a requirements analysis for the implementation projects and produce a requirements analysis document.
2. Given a set of informal specifications, produce a set of formal specifications for the same problem.

Connections:
   Related to: PL4, PL10, Se2
   Prerequisites: AL2
   Requisite for: SE4, SE5

The topics suggested for **SE3** are covered in Chapters 6 through 9 of SEPA. The majority of information on "informal specifications" can be obtained from Chapters 6 through 8. Formal specification is covered in Chapter 9. If formal specification is to be emphasized, additional outside readings are recommended (see Further Reading for Chapter 9.

SE4: Software Design and Implementation

Introduction to the principal paradigms that govern the design and implementation of large software systems.

Recurring Concepts: Complexity of large problems, conceptual and formal models, consistency and completeness, reuse.

Lecture Topics: (eight hours minimum)

1. Functional/ process-oriented design
2. Bottom-up design; support for reuse
3. Implementation strategies; e.g., top-down, bottom-up, teams
4. Implementation issues: performance improvement, debugging, antibugging

Suggested Laboratories: (open)

1. Do an object-based design for a given set of applications.

2. Implement the design from the above lab assignment.

3. Given a problem specification and a set of working modules with specifications, do a bottom-up design for the problem, applying as much reuse as possible.

4. Do a top-down implementation for a given software design.

5. Given a design and a partial top-down implementation perform the next step in the implementation.

Connections:
 Related to: PL11
 Prerequisites: AR2, DB1, SE2, SE3, PL2
 Requisite for:

The topics suggested for **SE4** are covered in detail throughout SEPA. Relevant SEPA chapters are noted in parentheses following the list of lecture topics:

1. Functional/ process-oriented design (SEPA Chapters 10 and 11)

2. Bottom-up design; support for reuse (SEPA Chapters 10 and 12)

3. Implementation strategies; e.g., top-down, bottom-up, teams (SEPA Chapter 19)

4. Implementation issues: performance improvement, debugging, antibugging (SEPA Chapters 10 and 19)

SE5: Verification and Validation

Introduction to methods and techniques for verification and validation of software systems.

Recurring Concepts: consistency and completeness, efficiency, trade-offs and consequences.

Lecture Topics (eight hours minimum)

1. Using pre- and postconditions, invariants, and elementary proofs of correctness

2. Code and design reading, structured walkthroughs

3. Testing; e.g., test plan generation, acceptance testing, unit testing, integration testing, regression testing

Suggested Laboratories: (open) Given a software specification, a piece of software, and a suite of test data, use verification and validation techniques to test the software and record findings.

Connections:
    Related to: PL4, PL5, PL10
    Prerequisites: SE3, Discrete Math (Logic and Proofs)
    Requisite for: SP3

The topics suggested for **SE5** are covered in detail throughout SEPA. Relevant SEPA chapters are noted in parentheses following the list of lecture topics:

1. Using pre- and postconditions, invariants, and elementary proofs of correctness (limited coverage in SEPA, Chapters 17 and 18, will need outside reading if this topic is to be emphasized)

2. Code and design reading, structured walkthroughs (SEPA Chapter 17)

3. Testing; e.g., test plan generation, acceptance testing, unit testing, integration testing, regression testing (SEPA Chapters 18 and 19)

4 GUIDELINES FOR UNIVERSITY COURSES

Courses in software engineering at both graduate and under-graduate levels are a necessary element of computer science and computer engineering curricula. In segment 3, the current ACM/IEEE Computing Curriculum was presented and an indication of how SEPA fits into it was provided.

When the first edition of SEPA was written (1981) few institutions offered software engineering courses. Today, things are different. Most schools offer at least one course in software engineering, and it may be that the design of your course is fixed. If so, the content of this segment of the *Instructor's Manual* may be of little interest. However, if you are considering the redesign of your course or are just starting one, the content of this segment may help.

In 1981, Elaine Kant (*ACM Software Engineering Notes*, August, 1981, vol.6, no.4, pp. 52-76) of Carnegie Mellon University published a detailed discussion of software engineering course design. Professor Kant gave me permission to include her paper in the *Instructor's Manual* for the first edition of SEPA. It is included with this edition because it is pragmatic and based on actual experience. It remains one of the best discussions of software engineering course design that I have encountered.

The Kant paper[1] (reproduced with permission) is presented in the following manner:

1. Reduced type font (i.e., reduced font) is used for all text reproduced directly from the Kant paper.
2. Normal type font is used to include my comments and supplementary notes.

You should note that parts of the Kant paper are direct extracts of student handouts and are therefore addressed directly

---

[1] Portions of the paper have been deleted for brevity.

to the student. Notes to the instructor (which do not appear in the actual handouts) are denoted with **boldface** font.

4.1 A SEMESTER COURSE IN SOFTWARE ENGINEERING
Elaine Kant, Carnegie-Mellon University

1. Introduction

Software engineering is a difficult subject to teach. The field is not a rigorous one, and there are few good textbooks [RSP note: hopefully, SEPA remedies this problem] or model courses to follow. To add to the confusion, the course is taught at many different levels to students with widely varying backgrounds. This paper discusses a project-oriented software engineering course aimed primarily at sophomores and juniors with at least two previous computer courses. Readings, suggested projects, and assignment descriptions are included. The course (called 15-311) has been taught at Carnegie-Mellon University for about five years. In 1980 and 1981 when the version described in this paper was taught, 133 students took the course. Over 50% of the students in these two years were sophomores, 25% were juniors, 10% seniors, and 10% graduate students, with a sprinkling of freshmen and special students. Nearly 80% of the students were mathematics majors (CMU has a software track in the mathematics program) and most of the other students majored in electrical engineering. The rest of this paper is a modification (what it should have been, rather than exactly what it was) of the handout given to the students on the most recent version of the class. It introduces the schedule of lectures and assignments for the project documentation. Comments for instructors are noted in **boldface** type.

RSP: Although Professor Kant indicates that the course has been designed for and taught to an undergraduate audience, there appears to be no reason why the same presentation (with added work and a bit more rigor) cannot be offered in a graduate curriculum.

2. Course Organization

This handout describes the course Software Engineering Methods. It explains the organization of the course, outlines the lecture topics and project assignment due dates, and gives some hints about working in groups and writing up the project documents. Finally, some suggested projects are given, and all of the assignments related to the project are described in detail.

2.1 Course Overview

Software engineering is concerned with long-term, large scale programming projects. This course introduces the topic through lectures and by giving you a chance to help design, manage, and implement a medium-sized project. The lectures and the group project will cover topics in software engineering management, problem specification and analysis, system design techniques, documentation, system testing and performance evaluation, system maintenance, reliable software, current programming and run-time environments, and possibilities for the future. The course will be difficult and time consuming, so you must have satisfied the prerequisites listed below.

2.2 Prerequisites

The prerequisite courses at CMU use Pascal and cover basic data structures (including a number of implementations for lists and sets), recursion, data abstraction, formal specification and verification, and finite state machine models. Prerequisites should probably also include a data structures course and an algorithms course and previous experience in writing small packages. I strongly recommend giving a pretest during the first week in class to make sure students have sufficient programming abilities. I gave out a questionnaire on programming background to help us spot potential strengths and weaknesses, but I had to take some of the answers with a grain of salt. For example, some students claimed to have written 106 lines of code!

Homework

Most homework will be related to the course project described below. There will also be reading assignments and occasional other exercises. There is an assignment writeup for each step of the project that includes a reading assignment. The readings should be done before you do the assignment. You are encouraged to read ahead as much as possible. Another course requirement is a weekly log of how much time you have spent on different activities related to the course. A sample log sheet is attached. You should turn in your log sheet each week at your section meeting.

The students generally do not like keeping logs. Although the logs gave me valuable feedback the first time I taught the course and although I think the students who kept them carefully learned from the experience, I'm not sure I believe they are critical. Perhaps they could be optional for extra credit.

Group Project

The class will be divided into groups of people. Students are strongly encouraged to form their own groups of compatible people. Projects normally will be selected from the list of suggested topics and be written in Pascal, but other projects can be negotiated. Each group will have regular weekly meetings with a "consultant" (a graduate student or member of the research staff) from the Computer Science Department. The projects will take most of the semester with major write-ups due at approximately two week intervals. There will also be some oral presentations, including a final demonstration of the project. Sample documents from the last course are on reserve in the library.

Five-person groups were chosen partly because of the large size of the class and partly to force students to face issues of project management. Smaller groups

would probably cause fewer problems but would teach fewer lessons about programming in groups. The last time I taught the class I scheduled two hours of lectures and made the section meeting the third class hour. It is important to impress on the students that these meetings are required and that they are if anything more important than the large lectures. Of course the success of this approach depends on having good teaching assistants, which I have been very fortunate to have.

RSP: Although allowing students to make-up their own teams ("groups") has definite advantages from the compatibility standpoint, it might be worthwhile to define teams based on the overall performance of individual students. If you take no part in defining the make-up of the teams, it is likely that you'll get one team of superstars and other teams with less capable performers. Distributing the superstars among various teams benefits everyone.

Tests and Individual Projects

There will be an in-class mid-term exam. Rather than a final, individual programming projects will be required during the last several weeks of class. The project will involve a modification or extension to a group project on a topic in software engineering.

I would suggest giving a final or second in-class test to make students read the second half of the textbook. There usually isn't much time for individual projects; if you want students to take them seriously you must make it clear to them that they are important.

Grades

About 50% of your grade will be based on the group project documents and demonstration. You are graded on the quality of the work you produce, not on how many hours a week you spend. Use your energy wisely! The rest of the grade will depend on individual tests, projects, and contributions to the group projects. It is very important that project assignments be turned in promptly, both to allow you time to complete the entire project on schedule and to allow us time to evaluate your work and make suggestions.

I strongly recommend insisting that the new students stick to a strict schedule. Groups that get more than a few days behind usually stay behind and never catch up. If a group is just lazy, insist that they turn things in on time and lower their grade if they don't; if their project is harder than it appeared at first, give them an extra week to figure out how to simplify it, but then insist that they stay on schedule. Also, make it very clear from the beginning that grades are not assigned in proportion to the number of hours spent or you will get a lot of complaints. Assigning individual grades in a projects course is difficult. I suggest stating exactly how much documentation and how many lines of debugged code, not counting comments and write-in statements, you expect from each person for an A, and what the grade penalties are for lateness and poor or incomplete documents. A reasonable breakdown for the grade might be 35% on whatever the group project as a whole deserves, 35% on the student's contributions to the project, and 30% on tests and individual projects. It is important to identify people who try to do their share as early as possible and convince them to shape up or drop the course, but this is difficult in practice.

RSP: I have found that the following method works well on team projects: A team leader is elected by the team within one week of the start of the project. (Kant discusses the leadership question later and I will make further comments at that time.) At monthly intervals, each member of the team submits a confidential rating sheet for all other members to the Professor. The grades submitted by the team leader receive extra weight. Poor individual performance is relatively easy to spot and a conference with offenders can be arranged if serious deficiencies are being reported.

Computer facilities

It is almost guaranteed that the computer will be heavily loaded and will crash at the most inconvenient times possible. Use autosave when editing, think before you write, code, or debug, and remember that the computing facilities you have here are as good as many you will find in "the real world," so don't think the situation will change when you get a job.

Comments from previous students ...

Warn people ahead of time what to expect... a lot of work is involved and anyone that doesn't have the time or perseverance should drop the course.
This has been the most worthwhile course I have taken since I learned to write in first grade.....I've learned a lot about computing, time management, people management, and my ability to stay logged in for days at a time. I even liked the course. There is only one major problem. My QPA is dropping faster than a wingless airplane because I've spent my semester working on 311.
CHORUS: This course is too much work!!!!

The course really was too much work for the number of units given.

Textbooks

RSP: For undergraduate courses, the only required textbook for my course is SEPA. However, like Professor Kant, I put a good selection of related texts on reserve at the library. See Appendix I of this Instructor's Manual for an extensive annotated bibliography. It would also be worthwhile for you to review the **References** and **Further Readings** sections at the end of each SEPA chapter and select appropriate library reserve books accordingly. Kant's required and recommended texts are dated and have not been reproduced.

Keeping a Log

Each person is to maintain a log of the time spent on course work and to break down the total time into categories. For example, categories might include time spent reading textbooks or articles, reading project problem descriptions, devising specifications, testing your program, etc.

Some of the numbers that students give seem a bit inflated, but in general they do spend an impressive amount of time on the course. Unfortunately a lot of time is wasted when the machine is heavily loaded.

We hope these logs will help you see how you spend your time and help you to make better predictions of the time needed by the different phases of a software project. Many companies in "the real world" actually require this sort of time-keeping.

RSP: The idea of a log is a good one. To help the students keep the log and to establish a format for data collection, it might not be a bad idea to provide each student with prepared "log entry sheets" so that the student need only fill in the blanks—a tabular format categorizing activities (with a mechanism for comments) is probably the best approach.

When in doubt, use as many categories as occur to you. You may want to compute the time breakdown in several ways for later summaries; for example, total computer time, or total time spent on the testing phase. Record daily use of CPU time as well as connect time and the time you spend thinking. You may want to make a special category for the time you spend in the computer center when you aren't really working on your project. When you make computer runs, record the reason for the run, the changes since the last run, and the result of the run. I think you will find this interesting to look back on and see how your time was spent and how it compares with your predicted times.

Comments from Previous Students

KEEP THE LOG SHEET. It may be a pain, but I wish I would have kept mine. It would be interesting to look back on it now and see how much time I really spent on the project in front of a terminal and how much I spent away from it.

3. Lecture Schedule

RSP: The schedule proposed by Kant assumes two lecture periods and a project session. At the University of Bridgeport, we meet once a week for a 2.5 hour lecture and allow students to schedule their own outside meetings. Frankly, I like the CMU approach better. Unfortunately, not all institutions have the resources (grad assistants, support faculty, etc.) to properly pull it off.

I believe that the schedule of topics proposed by Professor Kant could be improved somewhat. Alternative schedules are proposed in section 4.2 of this *Instructor's Manual* segment.

Week 1
Lecture: course overview, background questionnaire, possible pretest
Lecture: working in groups, management structures
Section: no meeting; students should be picking groups and projects

Week 2
Lecture: software requirements analysis, functional specifications
Lecture: Paradigms, common system organizations
Section: No meeting, but project/group proposals due

Week 3
Lecture: user interfaces, error/exception handling
Lecture: technical writing
Section: draft of functional specification due

Week 4
Lecture: abstraction in design
Lecture: modularity in design
Section: functional specification due

Week 5
Lecture: more on modules and abstraction
Lecture: more on modules and abstraction; families of systems
Section: top level code, overall design draft due

Week 6
Lecture: using libraries, journals, and references on algorithms
Lecture: checking interfaces, separate compilation Section: overall design specification due

Week 7
Lecture: reliability
Lecture: midterm exam
Section: interface definitions and stubs due

Week 8
Lecture: testing -- integration order, estimation, and scheduling
Lecture: testing -- individual module testing, test drivers
Section: detailed design specifications due, compiled module drivers due

Week 9
Lecture: discuss midterm, group interactions
Lecture: programming tools and environments for Pascal
Section: module top level code due

Week 10
Lecture: programming style, hints, and tricks
Lecture: more programming hints
Section: draft of test plan due

Week 11
Lecture: performance evaluation
Lecture: advances in programming environments (good debuggers, version control, syntactic editors
Section: test plan due, trade undebugged code

Week 12
Lecture: automated tools, program synthesis
Lecture: structure of organizations in the real world, types of jobs
Section: user manual due

Week 13
Lecture: computers and law
Lecture: computers and law
Section: practice demo

Week 14
Lecture: personal computers, networking
Lecture: project demonstrations

Week 15
Project demonstrations Final evaluation and individual projects due

4. Working in Groups

The students seem to feel that the groups won't be a problem in most cases, or don't want to face the issue early enough even if they have suspicions that there are problems in their group. I strongly recommend being very aware of group dynamics in the first few weeks of class. I will let the student experiences speak for themselves for the most part.

Most students prefer a democratic group organization. In a minority of groups, those in which all students have a reasonably equal commitment to the course, this can in fact work, as the following comments indicate:

. . . As a group, we did manage to work well without any strict leadership structure, partly because everyone was kept pretty well informed as to the work that was due. Also, everyone participated in the writing of all papers, no one person was dumped on. We each were given a section that was later critiqued and made a part of the total paper. I think that most groups would probably need some sort of structured management, but because of our group members' personalities, we worked well without any ....

. . . Our group worked together very well with no formal division of management. As in any society, there are leaders and there are followers. It seems that we had a good mix between leaders and followers.

However, most groups find they need some sort of leader; either because they all try to do everything and waste a lot of time arguing over details or because some people don't know what they should do unless someone gives them fairly explicit assignments. Some groups may want to have a design leader who is responsible for final technical decisions and a manager who is responsible for making sure everyone comes to meeting and does their share of the work. You may wish to have a permanent leader or to rotate leaders at different stages of the project (such as letting the editor for a document be the manager for that part of the project) Additional student comments follow:

. . . Unfortunately none of us had worked on a software team before. We were foolish and thought we could use the 5 - pointed star managerless technique where everyone talked to everyone and each did his equal share of each assignment. We realized pretty late in the game that this would not work ... any project group must have a leader or manager. The sooner the group realizes this the better off they'll be ... As few people as possible should write a particular document. One person (definitely not the author) should edit the entire document.

. . . The design process should, in my opinion, have a single person in charge of both the design and the paper. He should have final say in major disputes that seem to be unresolvable by any other course ... As many of the design decisions should be delegated as can be done reasonably... he must take care to limit the discussion of relatively minor points in order to keep the meetings from getting extremely long. Finally, let me say something about communication. In a word, you can't have enough.

While it is to be expected that some members of your group will be better writers, some better programmers, and so on, you are not to divide the labor on these grounds alone. This class is to be a learning experience, and each of you should get a substantial amount of practice in all of these areas, not just the ones you are already good at. Each person must write some of the documents, must edit one (see the next section), and must write code. You are not to turn one person into a full time typist and help - module writer just because you don't think their code will be perfect.

If one group member is a fantastic writer, by all means let him edit the first document and help teach the others how to write better. He might be assistant editor for some of the other documents, but he is not to write them all. If another member is a "wizard", go ahead and have her be design manager, but she is not to develop the software for the whole system, rather she should help the others improve their design and programming skills.

One problem that the students who were nominal leaders pointed out was that they had no power to back up the responsibilities that went with their authority. I don't have any good answers to this, except possibly to point out that the professor might believe this person's opinions about how much the other group members are contributing to the project. Another alternative is to get the TA to be a manager. To some extent this happened informally anyway, but I suspect it would require much more of a time commitment for them to take a formal leadership role.

RSP: The team approach to course projects is, as Professor Kant indicates, a difficult one to resolve. The following scheme tends to eliminate some, but not all, of the problems associated with "no-work team members" and a need for leadership authority:

1.   A team leader is elected by the team.
2.   Because the leader has more responsibility, she/he should receive rewards for good technical management and "take some of the flack" for a poor showing.
3.   Given the philosophy indicated in (2), the team leader will receive 1.10 of the overall team grade, if that grade is above 75% and no reward if the grade is below 75%.
4.   At monthly intervals, each member of the team submits a confidential rating sheet for other members. Comments of the team leader are weighted heavily in a final assessment.
5.   At the end of the project, a "bonus pool of points" (usually some percentage of the final grade) is distributed to team members based on the cumulative ratings.

This scheme tends to keep everyone actively involved in the project and provides the team leader with a "club" for those members who are not contributing.

5. General Comments on Documentation

This course involves a lot of writing. You are not being graded directly on your writing style, but good writing usually conveys ideas more clearly than poor writing, and the process of writing down your thoughts often clarifies them. Thus it is to your advantage to make the effort to organize your thoughts and write well, and we will often make comments about your style as well as about the project you are describing.

At the beginning of the semester you should skim all of the the assignments, then reread each several times before you begin to work on it. If you still have questions about the assignment after reading it carefully, be sure to ask your TA or the instructor.

You are to turn in two copies of each final document. One will be read by your TA and the instructor and will be returned to you with comments and a grade; the other will be kept in our files for future reference. Drafts of documents will only be read by your TA who will give comments but not a grade; you only need to turn in one copy for this.

Each document is to have one (not five!) editors, and each group member must edit one of the documents. Let us be very clear about what it means to edit a document. The editor has the final responsibility for turning in the document, sets deadlines for what the other members are to write, and may have to apply pressure to the other group members to do their part unless you have another manager for this.

To make things easier for you, we suggest you decide on a standard format (especially for the design documents). You may use the outline in the class directory as a model. Most of the assignments suggest an organization for the document. You do not need to follow it exactly if you have a better idea, but you should be sure to cover all the same material. Be sure to include acknowledgements at the end that say who wrote which sections and who the editor was.

I made up some grade sheets as guidelines for what to look for in evaluating the documents, but mostly they just reiterated the points made in the assignments, and I don't think it is worth reproducing them here.

RSP: The above material presents a good set of guidelines for students. I suggest that you require your students to follow predefined document outlines (outlines are provided in SEPA). First, this drives home the need for standardization in software engineering and second, it makes the task of reviewing and grading the documents much simpler.

You should save the best work from year to year so that over time, a sample "software configuration" can be provided as a guide for new students. I have found that outlines, in and of themselves, provide the students with inadequate guidance. Sample documents do a much better job.

6. Project Suggestions

Due Dates

Week 2: Turn in a description of the project you have chosen, one page minimum, five page maximum. Include a name for your group, a list of the names of the members, and a list of possible meeting times for your group. Include evening times; some TAs prefer them.

General Comments

Each group should select a project from the list given below; other project ideas may be used if approved by the teaching staff. A project should be feasible given the time constraints, but large enough that a cooperative team effort is required to complete it. Read the functional specification assignment and some of the others to get an idea of what will be expected of you. Note that you are asked to propose four increasingly difficult versions of your system. The first should be something you are sure you can do, and the last something you think you probably won't have time to finish. You should try to select a project that spans that range for your group.

After a group proposes a project, a teaching assistant should be assigned, and the TA and the instructor should give the group a critique of the proposal. Is it too ambitious or not enough? Are the goals clear? Can it be expanded or reduced later if necessary? Will it be possible to split it into smaller modules? The instructor should decide on the dates for each group's final demonstration fairly early in the semester so the group has a definite date to work towards.

Suggested Projects

A modest interactive editor. This could be a general text editor like Emacs or Fine [CMU editors], or it could be specific to some application.

This can range from very simple to very complex. Several groups built small editors as a minor part of other projects.

One interesting kind of special-purpose editor is designed for editing programs in, say, PASCAL. Special commands could, for example, insert a skeleton IF-THEN-ELSE or loop statement. Another might read the name of a variable "foo" and then insert "foo:=foo+1" into the program. A carefully designed editor might make it impossible to input a syntactically malformed program. Use your imagination.

As another example of an application-specific interactive editor, consider a font editor. A font is a set of 128 character definitions, where each character is a matrix of bits. The editor should make it easy to edit such matrices, to form new matrices by modifying old ones (once you get the letter "O" designed, you may want to use parts of it in "C", "G", "Q", and so on), to merge several matrices, and so on. This would involve both bookkeeping and some fancy terminal hacking. One group did a nice job on a font editor and processing routine to print files with font changes.A modest manuscript generator (something like a very simple version of Scribe [a CMU word processing system]).

A registrar's program to manage registration and scheduling, including printing student registration status, class lists for instructors, room use sheets, and process add-drop cards.

A program to teach arithmetic to a little brother or sister (i.e., a program for computer-aided instruction). This could include a scoring system, for example, and perhaps some analysis of errors to determine what kinds of problems to concentrate on. This is not a well-defined project and the group must be careful to decide what is to be handled.

A system to perform differentiation and simplification on symbolic expressions. Warning - simplification is quite tricky. I recommend encouraging groups to use existing algorithms first and then augment their programs. One group attempted this project and did a reasonable job with a pretty printing expression display and with function definitions but got bogged down on simplification. They had a hard time believing that simplification is in the eye of the beholder and the next step of the problem solving.

A database system, perhaps to maintain SCRIBE bibliography databases. This would make it convenient to add new entries to the database, along with key words, and also allow searching of the database, either by key word or by other fields, or with a special query language. Keep the on-line database alphabetized.

A database system for maintaining voting records of Federal and/or State Senators and Representatives. The system should keep all districts and their current representative along with their party, data of election, and a set of user-determined votes. There should be a way to score votes; for example, to determine how a person rates on a set of issues about the environment or the ERA or the space program. In the congressional record, votes recorded include yes, no, did not vote, paired for/against, unknown, etc. The user should be able to specify how these correspond to 1 or 0 or whatever for computing scores. There should be various ways to print out this information (again, perhaps with a query language), deal with people winning and losing elections, resigning, dying, etc.

A prototype simulation of a small, low-cost computing engine that one might find for sale in stores to the average consumer in the foreseeable future. It could be for children or adults; it might perform a common routine task now performed manually, or it might be a game. The Texas Instruments "Speak-and-Spell" ~(a registered trademark of Texas Instruments~) game would be one example.

A modest version of a game of Adventure or Dungeons and Dragons. The computer would serve as the dungeon-master. Alternatively, a game where the computer is a competitor or the board manager for a group of people. Depending on the game, an attractive display may be an important part of the project. Parker Brothers' "Clue" is an interesting game: you have to keep track of what other players know as well as what you know. Other possibilities are mastermind, checkers, bridge, backgammon, chess, and Go. Keep in mind that writing the programs to handle these games may not be nearly as fun or easy as playing them; certain of last year's students have threatened murder if anyone mentions the Rivets game to them again. Mastermind is perhaps too simple a project, checkers is a bit more complex but still pretty straightforward if existing approaches are used, and adventure games can be made reasonably difficult.

An <u>on-line recipe file and meal planner</u>. This could compute the overall nutrition value of a meal, summarize the necessary ingredients, and estimate cost. It might also be able to suggest a meal given "I want to use up this ground beef" or "I'm out of eggs and lettuce."

A <u>teacher's program to detect similarities in programs</u> (i.e., a "cheat detector"), for programs of about the size and complexity required for week long homework assignments.

A <u>program version comparator and updater</u>. This is like the previous suggestion, but the emphasis is on determining differences rather than similarities. One might use this system after a day's editing, to get a summary of all changes. Suppose that two people edit the same program, adding different fancy features. This system might determine the differences between them and automatically or (more likely) interactively merge them to produce a new program with the features of both.

An <u>automated bank teller</u>. This would keep track of accounts, and let users perform various transactions: shuffle money between accounts, make deposits and withdrawals, pay bills (manually or automatically), include a display similar to the ones at the real money machines, etc. The system should be resistant to abuse and should be reliable (able to keep everyone's money straight in spite of system crashes). This is a simple project unless it includes features like multiple tellers and simultaneous deposits and withdrawals, bank manager programs, and good backup systems.

A <u>PASCAL syntax and pretty-print checker</u>. This would read a PASCAL program and perform various syntax checks, and in particular check that the program indentation matched the syntax. One might get output such as this:
```
procedure foo(a b:real);
            ^ ** Missing comma
  begin     if a > 0.0 then b := a else b := - a;
    *** ELSE farther left than matching IF
  a := a / 2.0
end;
  ^ ** END not aligned with BEGIN
```
An ambitious version of this would attempt to correct errors (perhaps just indentation errors).

A <u>string handling package</u>. This would provide dynamic allocation of variable-length character strings, with either explicit or automatic de-allocation. In addition to managing storage, the package should include facilities for operating on strings (copying, concatenating, comparing, sorting, searching, matching, etc.). This project is straightforward but can involve a lot of work, especially if fancy pattern matching is attempted. One group did a nice job on a moderately sized string package.

A complex string-matching package, expanded into a spelling and diction checker. (The string matching might be based on regular expressions a la Aho). It could check a document for commonly misspelled words, as well as instances of such redundant fragments as "-ing behavior", "added increment", and so on.

A personal finances manager. Something to balance the checking account, keep track of bills, match receipts to credit card statements, do taxes, provide summary reports in various categories, and so on. One group did a modest version of this.

A simulator, with debugging aids, for some interesting computer (8080, PDP-11, M68000 or whatever). [RSP note: Needless to say, these machines should be updated to reflect current technology!] Many groups have done simulator/debugging systems. They seem to be reasonable size projects if the instruction set is not very large, and the project can be extended to include fancy displays and so on.

An interpreter for (a subset) of Pascal [or Ada]. An interactive debugger for such an interpreter. An interpreter written in Lisp may be available.

A calendar maintainer. This would schedule your time, send reminders when necessary (through the computer mail system), perhaps coordinate with other people's calendars for scheduling meetings, and so on. Printing parts of the calendar on demand is a must ("What's up for today?" or "Let's see next week at a glance." or "What in the world was I doing last Tuesday?" or "On what day of the week for the next four weeks is there an hour free starting at 10:00?").

On a similar theme, a terminal reservation system for a terminal room. This would be an automated sign-up sheet for a collection of terminals (and possibly other resources). People should be able to express preferences for various times. The system should include facilities for administrators to collect and print statistics on usage as well as a scheduling algorithm to ensure fair distribution of resources among users. It should be easy to change the scheduling algorithm. (Ignore the fact that you need to use a terminal to sign up for a terminal! For example, assume that one is reserved for this purpose.)

A verification condition generator.

A tree (or graph) structured bulletin-board system, with the root allowed in any user's directory. Any user could post notices for others to read. Notices (especially replies) could be associated with other notices (hence the graph structure). A user might want to ask such questions as "which notices of mine have had answers attached that I haven't read yet?" Some branches of such a bulletin board might serve as a structured on-line documentation system. This would have to have a nice user interface; it should also lead the beginner by the hand (possibly by guiding them through a documentation tree!) A stripped-down version of the user interface for hard-copy terminals should be a part of the core system. One group tried a similar project but was overly ambitious and had trouble completing the project.

Write <u>a program for analyzing the NFL playoff situation</u>, which has a complex set of rules for resolving various situations that can arise. One portion of the project would be an evaluator to determine the playoff choices given the end-of-season scenario. The rules should be modularly implemented so that they can be changed (as they frequently are). The user interface could vary from something simple to a system capable of answering questions like "If Pittsburgh loses to Houston, what must occur for Pittsburgh to enter the playoffs?" (expressed in some more formal notation). Incremental improvements might include something like the capability to guess, based on the season record so far, how some upcoming games might be decided or what games might be crucial.

A <u>package for handling file I/O</u>. You could build on some of the existing packages, perhaps adding routines for scanning and parsing file names and switches for different machines. For example, you could write routines to extract information from a specification such as:

DEVICE: NAME.EXT(P,PN) <protection>/
switch: ()/switch.

You might have an iterator that returned the next switch each time it was called.

<u>Other possibilities</u> are limited only by your imagination. While projects such as display and window packages, command interpreters, and general menu handling systems would be quite feasible, some projects such as a poem or music composer or simple language translator or simple theorem prover boarder on research topics and you will have to be very careful not to waste all your time fighting about what you are going to do or which of the many possible approaches you will take. We want you to have a chance to complete a project, not just start one.

RSP: Some of the projects noted above are somewhat frivolous, but all will serve to demonstrate software engineering methodology.

It is often worthwhile to poll various departments at your institution for small, but "real," projects that students might attempt. If you do this, your students will get to communicate with real customers and the results of their work may have lasting benefit. Be careful here, however, there is a tendency to bite off more than your students can chew!

With the increasing emphasis on CASE, you might consider assigning simplified software engineering tools as projects:

- a complexity calculator (McCabe's metric) for small programs
- a PDL to flowchart generator
- a simple test case generator
- a tool to assist in maintenance record keeping
- an automated software costing tool
- a computer graphics based DFD generator
- a decision table processor
- an automated productivity record keeping system
- a reverse or re-engineering tool for unstructured code
- a tool to assist in statistical quality assurance
- a tool to assist in risk analysis for project planning
- a tool to generate notation for OOA and/or OOD
- a tool that will perform a grammatical parse on English language narrative and extract objects and operations

The difficulty of each of the above projects can be tuned to the sophistication of the students and the number of people on a team. For many of these, the students will have to "learn ahead" for topics that are not discussed until late in the course.

First Reading Assignment

SEPA assignment: See alternative course outline presented in section 4.2 of the *Instructor's Manual*.

7. Functional Specification Assignment

Due Dates

Week 3 draft of the paper described here; week 4 final version of paper, hand in two copies, one returned with comments, one for our files.

General comments on the assignment

It is very important for the students to make definite commitments about what their project will involve. Insist on a draft and make them rewrite the final version if necessary. Points to stress are: coming up with realistic versions of the system for the "plain and fancy" section; writing samples of the system behavior, and making sure the functional specification is a very good first step towards the user manual.

The main purpose of the Functional Specification is to explain what you are going to do for your project as opposed to how you will accomplish these goals. The functional specification, coupled with a management plan (which we will not write up formally) and an overall design (which will be your next assignment), describe the proposal to your client. When accepted, these documents are a contract between you and your client (the teaching staff) about what you intend to deliver. Changes can be negotiated later and should be recorded as an appendix to this document. When writing this paper, therefore, you should keep in mind that your audience will be a client (who, in general, is not an expert in computer science) and your group members, who will want to refer back to this document periodically to be reminded of what they are supposed to be doing. The fact is that in this course your clients are computer scientists and that your document will be graded might encourage you to think and write as carefully as possible.

RSP: It is important to have each team develop an abbreviated Software Plan for the project they undertake. The plan should emphasize scheduling, in fact, you should insist that each team develop a week by week schedule and encourage them to schedule on a daily basis for 7 to 10 days in advance. It is critically important to have the students assign responsibilities within the team. If possible, it would be nice to provide the students with a scheduling tool (e.g., MacProject II) that will make this effort a bit easier.

Cost estimation is not nearly as important in this context, but you can provide data for LOC costing and suggest the use of an empirical model such as COCOMO to help in estimating.

Discuss what you want your system to look like and produce as many examples as possible of its behavior. In your group meetings you can take turns playing different roles. One person could be the system user, one could play the system, one could be system implementer and make sure the "system" is feasible, one could be the group facilitator. In your group meetings you can take turns playing different roles. One person could be the system user, one could play the system, one could be system implementer and make sure the "system" is feasible, one could be the group facilitator.

Contents of a Functional Specification

Title Page

This assignment, as well as all others throughout the year, should be turned in with a title cover or cover page that includes the following information:

- A title that identifies the document

- The name of your group (such as "Great Hacks, Inc.")
- The people who contributed to this document
- Course name, instructor's name, TA's name, date

Functional Summary

In about 2 pages, you should briefly summarize the project you are working on. Give your system a name. Describe what it does and who will use it. What needs will your system satisfy? How will it help the users? Outline the most important features of your system. Describe the physical environment in which your system will be used, including any other systems with which the new system will interface. Are there any important performance goals for your system: time or space efficiency, security, or reliability?

Details concerning system user interactions

The main point of this section (which should be approximately ten pages) is to describe the functions that the system will perform from the point of view of the system user. You need to cover the kinds of inputs your system expects, the actions it will take on both expected and unexpected inputs, and the types of outputs that the user will see in those cases. Part of this section will eventually be developed into a user manual. First we'll consider the content, then the form, of these descriptions.

The inputs, state changes, and outputs should be described in reasonable detail. You need not stick to the exact wording of messages, but you should make definite statements. You can negotiate major changes later. Describe what legal values or ranges your system will accept for inputs, what precision or accuracy constraints you will follow, and how you will handle errors.

Your functional description should employ some of the following techniques:

Sample transcript . A very important part of the description is a sample interaction with the system in the form of a transcript of a dialogue between a user and the system. Use upper and lower case or some similar convention to distinguish between what the program types and what the user types.

Students resist doing this, but I would insist that they produce a number of examples.

RSP: I have each team develop a "paper prototype" of the system that they are to build. This is particularly useful for graphics applications but has benefits for all types of projects. One way to overcome students' resistance is to convince them that the prototype will be a useful artifact if disaster strikes and they can't get their application "up and running." In recent years, a number of students have develop Macintosh Hypercard prototypes and a few have extended these into reasonably sophisticated "applications." I see no reason to resist this, as long as analysis, design and testing are conducted appropriately.

FSM model . If your system can be thought of as being in a number of states, you can draw a finite state machine model (FSM). The different states might correspond to different prompts for user response that are shown in your dialogue.

BNF specification . If much of your system involves commands specified by the user, write a BNF describing the syntax of these commands.

Boxes, arrows, and tables . As appropriate, use pictures of equipment, data flow or control flow diagrams, decision tables, etc. Be sure that any diagrams are captioned and that there is a key explaining what various boxes and arrows mean.

Glossaries . Be sure that all specialized terms are defined in the body of the document or in a collection at the end. This could include computer science terms that you wouldn't expect your client to know or application terms (from accounting, geology, or whatever) that programmers working on the project might not understand.

Feasibility

Make sure your project has a chance of being completed in a semester. What are your preliminary thoughts on how you will break down the different features of the project? What are the major classes of functions and the relationships between them? Think a little about your main data structures and algorithms, and spend a page or so discussing possible implementations. Don't waste a lot of time fighting over details, but be sure to ask your TA or the instructor if you aren't sure how hard something will be.

Our system, plain and fancy

Predicting how much can really be accomplished in a finite period of time is often tricky. It is important to decide what a bare bones version of your dream would involve. Describe, in one or two pages, the composite of your skeletal system. What functions will not be included, and why? Cover yourself by making sure that reading between the lines doesn't make your customer think that more is being promised than you plan to deliver. Now sketch out which features will be added as time permits. Try to organize the bells and whistles into packages that could be added independently or in some predictable order. Also think about the order in which parts of the system can be dropped so that you can retreat gracefully if necessary. (You may wish to look ahead at the Parnas readings listed in the design document handout to find out more about subsetting.)

A good way to describe your series of systems is in the form of user reference cards. You should make a series of three or four cards outlining what is

contained in (or added by):
- a kernel system with absolutely minimal features (that you are positive you can finish in 3/4 of a semester)
- a cheap but usable system (that you expect to finish)
- a standard system (that you have a good chance finishing)
- a super system (that you probably won't be able to finish but would like to; don't make this something impossible though)

Summary

Don't drop the reader off a cliff at the end of your paper. It's been a long time since the beginning of the paper. Restate the main points you want remembered.

Acknowledgements

Write down the authors of individual sections, the editor of the whole paper, outside consultants,etc. (Do this for all future papers as well.) This will help people figure out who to ask for more details.

RSP: I try to emphasize to the students that all documentation should stand on its own—that is, they should not assume that "We'll be around to answer any questions, so we can be sloppy about ambiguity, etc."

Optional Sections

A real functional specification would include a number of items that you may wish to skip at this point. Some of them require more experience to predict and may be covered later, some are not relevant to all projects, and some have already been discussed. Use your good judgement.

- Make some general statements about the performance goals for your system. What are your goals for system run time, main and disk memory use? What kind of reliability will you guarantee? Security of information? What kind of performance trade-offs have you decided to make?
- Can you say anything about compatibility with existing software or hardware? What about an installation agreement? Maintenance contract?
- What resources are to be committed to the project? Who are the people on the project? Their skills and background? What is the promised delivery date? How much computer time and space will be used to develop the project?
- What publications will be produced? Who are the intended audiences?

Readings

SEPA assignment: See alternative course outline presented in section 4.2 of the *Instructor's Manual*.

Some comments by previous students

. . . Writing down the functional specifications is fundamental to having a good start on a well-designed project. No matter how much you discuss something there will be loose ends and not until you write your ideas down will these unresolved parts become visible. The most important sections of the paper are those dealing with the functions of the system. You need to understand thoroughly "the transformations from the user point of view." You should not have vague points unless you absolutely cannot help it.

. . . In some respects the Functional Specification was the most useful of the documents. It forced the group to adopt a rigid management structure (we quickly found that five people writing the document causes tremendous amounts of bickering) and outlined the goals of the project. It also provided a first look at the more serious problem which the project would have to overcome.

8. Design Documents

Due dates

Week 5.   bring in top-level code and design draft; divide responsibilities for overall design sections
Week 6.   overall design specifications due (2 copies) (preliminary grade) reapportion responsibilities, group review
Week 7.   interface definitions and stubs due (preliminary grade)
Week 8.   detailed design specifications due (2 copies) major grade) module drivers for kernel system due (compiled but not tested) reapportion and review remaining tasks in section

The design process

The design of large systems is still a bit of an art. To put a little order into the chaos, we've established a few milestones for you. During the design process you should focus on the parts of the design essential to producing a core system and merely outline extensions to a more complete system. One of your major goals is to get something working by your deadline, even if it isn't the full system. Thus, you should determine what needs to go into a skeletal system and schedule the design of those components first.

The end goal in the design process is a detailed design document that is complete enough to be a reference from which any competent [software engineer] computer scientist can produce code, test plans, or a user manual. (This document should eventually evolve into the code and system maintainers' guide.)

An intermediate goal is the overall design specification. This can be considered a draft of the detailed design document with some of the details missing. Interfaces between modules should be clearly defined.

Once the design has been written down, everyone in the group should read the entire document to make sure they understand the design. Individuals should be assigned responsibility for particular modules and should design these in more detail.

Each person should carefully review at least one other person's section (and all sections should be reviewed by someone other than the author). Pick the one(s) with which your module has the strongest interaction(s). Based on the examination on the module interactions, you should prepare a set of interface definitions.

The final step is then to prepare the detailed design document. Most of the work will be done by individuals filling in the details of their modules, but you must review the document as a whole to make sure people are using the same interface definitions and to make sure that everything has been covered and that the parts of the document hang together.

RSP: SEPA introduces a review technique that can be applied by the students during design. You should encourage the use of walkthroughs. Be sure that students apply a formal (data flow, data structure or object-oriented) design technique. A preliminary design "review"—a 15 minute in class design presentation by each team—is recommended during the early weeks of design.

Writing the documents

First of all, remember Brook's comment (The Mythical Man-Month, page 165):

Most documentation fails in giving too little overview. The trees are described, the bark and leaves are commented, but there is no map of the forest. To write a useful prose description, stand way back and come in slowly.

Your goal should be to provide a recursive (top down) description of your program in a form something like the following. You probably won't be able to design your project completely top down, but such a description should be a good explanatory and reference tool.

For each level, you should cover the following:

Abstract—What services does this program, module, routine, etc. provide to outsiders?

Implementation Documentation—Are any special instructions need for the system user; for the writer of other modules?

Design—What is the basic design of this module or routine? How are the design decisions reflected in the submodules or routines which make up the whole? How are the pieces combined to accomplish the main function described in the abstract?

Exports—What routines does this (sub)module make available to other modules? What type declarations? What constants? (Remember, types can be exported, but not parameters.)

Imports—What procedures defined in other modules are used? (Beware: a procedure, function, or type cannot be both an import and an export of the same module!).

Input/output—Make sure all necessary actions are specified.

Subparts—What are the names of the submodules, routines, and/or data abstractions that make up the module or submodule?

Pre and Post conditions—What are the pre and post conditions on the main routines in your module? What are the important invariants on your data structures?

Error Handling—What is the range of legal values? What happens when other values are found? Test Cases -- List all your fiendish ideas for cases that might break the system or module or routine. If you do a good job here, you will be more sure of having a good design and most of your test plan will be already written.

Concrete Implementation—For (sub)modules that are data abstractions, give the concrete representation (Pascal declaration) here; the access functions will be listed as subparts. For routines, this is where the code goes. Make clear what data structures are private to the module. Define any technical terms relevant to the module.

Side Effects—Hopefully there aren't any, but if there are, you'd better make them explicit.

Miscellaneous—Just in case you think of anything else (for example, an estimate of how frequently various routines might be used or how much code will have to be written), throw it in!

Obviously, not all categories are needed at all levels. For access routines, for example all that is needed maybe a good function declaration. (Also, please don't call all of your procedures modules!) Where appropriate, write your description in Pascal or in a formal high-level language.

RSP: In the above discussion, Kant uses terminology that is specific to her course. Refer to SEPA, Chapter 10, for a discussion of recommended design document format. I would recommend against using the above section verbatim (as a handout) in that conflicting terms may cause some confusion.

The Overall Design Document (discussed below) is the equivalent of the preliminary Design Document discussed in SEPA. Emphasis here should be on program structure, interfaces and data structure.

Overall Design Document

For the overall design document, you should define your major data abstractions and modules, focusing on the abstract, design, and submodules, and on error handling and exports and imports of the major modules. When in doubt about whether something belongs in the overall or detailed design, put it in the overall design with a note that you aren't sure. Fill in as many other details as possible -- it will be to your advantage to see it all in writing and get some feedback from yourselves and the teaching staff. You should also include sections discussing the modification and the management questions. The document should be about 30 - 50 pages. A table of contents is a must for this document, and an index would be helpful.

Detailed Design Document

The detailed design document should include answers to all of the questions for as many levels as possible. You do not have to write the code to do this, but there may be some modules for which the clearest way to explain the function is to write an outline of the code. This is acceptable if the code is written in terms of calls to other high-level functions (no bit-twiddling) and is easy to read. Update the sections describing coding responsibilities. A table of contents and an index are necessary in this document. If your document seems to be getting too long (more than 75 - 100 pages) consult your TA. Good luck!

Readings

SEPA assignment: See alternative course outline presented in section 4.2 of the *Instructor's Manual.*

Comments from previous students

. . . The specifications were extremely helpful when designing the code. Our specifications were detailed enough that attempting to write a piece of code for a module could almost be taken directly out off of the specifications. Writing the design specifications twice helped us a great deal. Many things were pointed out to us that needed improvement, and the second set of specifications gave us time to think things out a little longer.

. . . Every time I violated the principles of abstract design, I suffered. Abstract data types, modular decomposition, and information hiding can really work. The design process was definitely a major factor in simplifying the debugging process. It is interesting to note that we had almost no interface errors. We attribute this to good communication within the group.

9. Testing Plans Assignment

Due Dates

Week 9.   top level code for main modules, tested with drives and stubs, due
Week 10.   test plan document due

Overview

About this time students often start to fall behind or decide that the test plan isn't important. All I can suggest is making sure they stay on time beforehand or

having them write test schedules as part of the design document.

Testing is an important part of a software project. The software team must therefore carefully plan and document the order in which modules are to be integrated and the order in which the individual modules are to be completed and tested in isolation. Testing and debugging methods must also be agreed upon, documented, and eventually carried out. The grade you get on the test plan is tentative; a final grade will be assigned after you complete the testing process.

The purpose of a test plan document is to convince the management (in this case, the teaching staff) that a feasible test plan has been designed and also to provide the project members with directions for the testing phase of the project. This assignment outlines some constraints on the test plans. Several stages of tests must be scheduled, and several testing procedures must be explored. Scheduling is required for unit tests, integration testing, functional testing, performance evaluation, and an acceptance test (the demonstration). These tests must include practice in the techniques of walkthroughs, extensive logic testing, input/output testing, and optionally verification. The following sections give details of the contents and style of the test plan document, and the final section lists some reading material that should help you design a better test plan.

Design the test plan

The test and evaluation plan should contain the following components: statements of objectives and success criteria, integration plan, testing and evaluation methodologies, and responsibilities and schedules. These components are described in more detail below.

1. Objectives and Success Criteria: The test plan document should contain a statement of the overall testing objectives and the objectives of the individual tests that are planned.

2. Integration Plan: An important decision to be made about testing is the order in which modules are to be combined and therefore the order in which they will be tested individually. You must plan for individual module tests, the combination of modules during integration testing, a functional test, and an acceptance test (the demo).

The test plan document should describe and defend your integration method. The "big bang" method of integration is not acceptable, but many variants or combinations of top down and bottom up integration are acceptable if convincingly defended.

3. Testing Methodologies: You should design a plan to test all of the modules of your system. Your test plan document should name at least one module to which each [testing] technique is to be applied; you may decide the testing technique for the other modules later on. Each person on the software team is to perform at least one set of tests and turn in a couple of pages describing the process at a later date.

4. Responsibilities and Schedules: The test plan should provide a schedule describing dates and responsibilities.

- First, determine an order in which to perform integration and functional tests. In scheduling, you should make use of the dependency graphs based on the external functions that the modules require.

- Next, this order should be used to determine the order in which the individual modules are to be tested. Determine the dates by which tests are to be completed and the individuals responsible for the testing. Prepare a master test plan schedule and include it in the document.

- Finally, you must define a monitoring procedure to ensure that tests are designed and carried out on schedule. Someone will have to keep a notebook and report lack of compliance to the other team members. Similarly, there must be a procedure for reporting and correcting bugs.

Writing the document

The test plan document is to contain an introductory section that summarizes the whole document in a page or two and discussion sections that cover the plans in more detail. A total number of pages between 15 and 25 is about right.

Remember that this document is intended for several audiences. The document should be organized so that it is easy to find schedule summaries and monitoring plans and easy directions on their personal responsibilities. The test plan should not be very long; if you find that the writing of the document is taking significantly longer than the design of the test plan, consult a member of the teaching staff. Representative samples of your tests are to be turned in later (as scheduled in the test plan).

The introductory section of the test plan document, which should only be about three pages long, should include the following:

- Overall objectives and success criteria
- Summary of the integration plan -- a list of tests and dates and people responsible
- Summary of the module-to-test-technique mapping for the four required testing techniques
- Summary of the monitoring, reporting, and correcting procedures
- Proposed dates for submission of individual test reports

The discussion sections should contain:

- Defense for the integration plan (about half a page)
- Details of the tests with objective and success criteria for each test or group of tests (assuming you have proposed most of the tests in your design document, there should not be more than 20 entries in this list, and each entry should be less than one page long; if you did not have good tests in your design document however, you should include them here)
- Details of the tests with objectives and success criteria for each test or group of tests (assuming you have proposed most of the tests in your design document, there should not be more than 20 entries in this list, and each entry should be less than one page long.
- Details of monitoring, reporting, and testing procedures (a page or so

should suffice)

- Details of individual team member assignments (just a page or so, this is basically a cross reference list.

Readings

SEPA assignment: See alternative course outline presented in section 4.2 of the *Instructor's Manual*.

Comments by Previous Students

... we proposed to implement on a few functions in various categories, but instead actually tried to implement all. As a result, it was difficult to test the integrated system. It would have been better to try running a small system which handled all modes, rather than a large one that was buggy ... design was generally adaptable to the smaller, more complete system and certainly wasn't responsible for hindering us from building it.

10. User Manual

Week 11.   draft due
Week 12.   final version due

This document should be a self contained description of how to use your system. A user manual should be a polished, professional piece of technical prose that a software company is proud to have accompany one of their products. (And it is a handy accomplishment to show off at job interviews!)

The document should have a structure that is evident to someone who is reading it straight through and someone looking for a particular topic or fact. A table of contents is required, and the organization that it reflects should be considered carefully. An index and Appendices might also be helpful.

Remember that the document should be completely self explanatory. Do not assume the reader has your functional specification. You may of course edit the sections of prose from your previous documents. Do not discuss any implementation unless it directly affects the user's interface with the system.

RSP: I suggest to students that any interactive system, if properly designed, should be capable of being used without repeated and heavy *User Manual* references. If you haven't done so already, this might be a good place to discuss key aspects of HCI.

In my opinion, the single most important part of the User Manual is the Index. Even if your students do not have the tools to develop one, you should emphasize its importance. In fact, if you don't have an indexing tool, this might be an excellent course project.

Your User Manual should be no longer than 25-30 pages. A short command summary or pocket reference card might also be useful.

Your document ought to cover the following list of topics. The exact order in which you present material and whether certain topics are combined should be dictated by your particular project and your own writing style.

Introduction—a concise statement of what your program does, possibly including motivation and philosophy.
How to use your system—an overall description of the style of user interaction, device constraints and any arbitrary design choices you made that the user ought to know about.
Detailed system operation—an organized list of all use commands and when they are appropriate; some examples might be helpful [RSP note: mandatory in my courses!] A section for novices and experts are also possibilities.
Error recognition and handling—what to expect and what to do.
An extended example—show exactly what the user does and how the computer responds. Use appropriate conventions to indicate user actions and computer responses.
A *list of known "features"* [actions that some would call bugs!] and deficiencies

Everyone complains about how cryptic computer manuals are. This is your chance to show us what a good manual looks like.

RSP: In her original paper, Professor Kant goes on to say that she has mixed emotions about the *User Manual* indicating that students rush through it and often write what they hope the system will do as opposed to what it really does. On the other hand, learning how to properly prepare this form of documentation is one of the most valuable lessons for a budding software engineer. I would recommend attaching a reasonably heavy grade weight to this document—thereby forcing students to focus on it.

11. Demonstration

You should prepare about 15 minutes of material that exhibit the best features of your system and allow about five minutes for questions and feedback from the audience. If your system has been properly debugged, you can let the audience tell you what to type to show off your error handling and user help facilities. Because time is so short, it is important to practice what you are going to say and do. You should give one practice demo to your TA about one week beforehand.

Twenty minutes is not nearly enough time to do the demo properly, but it's enough time to give the other students a flavor for what has been done. Many of the groups gave another demo outside class so that there was enough time to find out how their system really performed. The deadline for the demo seemed

to be a good forcing function for most students; without it, I suspect that many students would never finish their project.

12. Final Project Evaluation

I didn't give these a letter grade but did insist that they turn them in. I find the feedback helpful (and a good source of quotations!) and believe it gives the students a chance to express their feelings about the course.

The purpose of this document is to evaluate your final project. The document provides an opportunity to step back and put things in perspective and appreciate how much you have accomplished. If your group doesn't agree on the evaluation and recommendations, feel free to write individual versions.

Code and Demo Description

You should turn in the complete code for your system and a transcript of your demo along with the rest of the evaluation.

Functional Performance

Discuss how well your project satisfies your original functional specifications. What has been added or subtracted? What advice would you give next year's students about writing functional specifications? Suggest improvements to the assignment description.

Compare the actual performance of your system to the predicted performance (LOC, memory requirement, response times, calculation times, etc.). Can you come up with reasons for the discrepancies (if any)?

The Design Process

Were you satisfied with your design process? How helpful was the process of writing out the specifications? How would you go about the design process next time? What differences, if any, would you propose for the overall and detailed design assignments?

Testing

Did the order of integration that you chose seem to work out reasonably well? Did you stick to your test plan schedule? If not, why, and what would you change if you had to do it again? What method did you use for recording test results?

Was debugging easier or harder than you expected? Do you think that the design process significantly reduced the amount of time needed for coding and debugging? Discuss the types of bugs you encountered. Were they limited to one module? The result of errors in the interface specifications? How did you handle fixing bugs?

Management

What was the real management structure within your group? Does it bear any resemblance to the structure that you had planned? Did you have any problems getting people to do their share of the work? Do you have any suggestions on how this could have been handled better?

Compare the actual time spent designing, coding, testing, debugging, and managing the project with your predicted times. Break this down by individual modules and individual people. Have you learned anything that will help you to make better predictions next time? What would you suggest to next year's students?

The Real World

Discuss what you might have done differently if this were a real world project. How much additional work would be required to complete the project to the level described in the functional specification? How much would you consider selling the system for? Do you think the system is worth its cost?

Recommendations for Next Year

What changes would you suggest for next year? Be more specific than "less work." Try to summarize what you have learned and which aspects of the course were most helpful. Which would you suggest shortening or eliminating? What changes or scheduling would you suggest? Were the regular weekly meetings with the TAs helpful? Would you recommend easier projects, or would you rather start with more specific specifications and decomposition, or would you rather not choose your own projects? What about the number of people in the group? Any other topics that you would like to have covered (or ignored)?

13. Alternate Course Organizations

The course as it is currently organized is really too much work for one semester. It should get more credits for being a lab course or be split into two semesters. If there were two semesters, the first could be spent on the readings and on writing a very small system or a module for a system to learn about abstraction. This would also allow students to read about testing beforehand so that they can plan the design and implementation schedule for easy testing.

Another organization, which is unlikely at most schools, is to have a full semester schedule of software engineering -- a total immersion experience. This would involve a team teaching effort with lecture on technical writing and more serious grading of the assignments for writing style, a social psychology course focusing on the interactions of small groups (or a management course), and another set of computer science lectures on algorithms and data structures (or perhaps on compilers and operating systems.

Concluding Comments

RSP: The course described by Professor Kant is an ambitious undertaking. The project flavor is essential for a complete understanding of software engineering, but the time pressure and demands of other courses may blunt its impact. It is possible to conduct the course with a series of controlled "mini-projects," each addressing one key software engineering activity, and still get all important points across.

Ideally, the course should span two terms—the first emphasizing readings and lectures and the second dedicated to a full term project (with necessary oversight). Such a course would be ideal for a senior year in CS or computer engineering, providing the student with a real world project flavor before he/she graduates.

Some professors have told me that they assign all reading in SEPA (the entire book!) during the first four to six weeks of a term, enabling students to get a feel for all aspects of software engineering. Lectures are paced throughout the term and the project commences immediately after the "reading period." I've never tried this, but everyone who has reports uniformly good results. Note: The third edition of SEPA is almost 40 percent longer than the first. Certainly, a lot of reading in four weeks!

Kant's paper doesn't mention a number of important topics that should be covered in every software engineering course and encouraged in all projects. Project planning, elements of system engineering and software maintenance and SCM are important for all young software engineers to understand. Course content should include them! Formal technical reviews (walkthroughs) are an essential SQA mechanism. You should encourage your students to conduct them as part of their projects by requiring that Technical Review Summary Reports be submitted as part of the project deliverables.

Another topic missing in Kant's paper (understandably, given the scarcity of tools at the time she wrote it) is the application of CASE tools to aid in course project work. Using the *Software Engineering Teaching System* (described in Segment 2 of this *Instructor's Manual*, you now have the ability to demonstrate tools and also have them available (on a limited basis) for student projects).

You should note that software engineering courses can be successfully conducted without TAs and with somewhat less ambitious project goals. The design of your course should, of course, be guided by the backgrounds, interests and capabilities of your students. However, the overall framework proposed by Kant can serve as an excellent foundation.

4.2 ALTERNATIVE COURSE DESIGNS USING SEPA

The third edition of SEPA has been designed to accommodate a number of different approaches for teaching software engineering. The book has been partitioned in a manner that will enable you to use it for courses with the following emphasis:

- a general course in software engineering
- a course that emphasizes methods
- an analysis oriented course
- a design oriented course
- a management oriented course

In the sections that follow, course schedules, readings and other suggestions are provided for each of these courses.

4.2.1 A General Course in Software Engineering

A general course in software engineering is what I call a "soup to nuts" course. It introduces the student to all important aspects of the discipline, but of necessity, does not go into depth in every one. The schedule that follows is based on a 14 week term and assumes the use of SEPA as a required course text. The chapters of SEPA follow the lecture presentations closely; reading assignments from SEPA and other books are implied by the lecture topic; homework problems, if assigned, may be found at the conclusion of each chapter in SEPA.

Project deliverables should be distributed evenly throughout the term. In-class reviews are desirable but time pressure may cause problems if they are conducted.

Week 1   The impact of software
            The software crisis and the "aging software plant"
            An overview of software engineering
            Discussion of project requirements and topics
            Planning software project—an introduction

Readings: SEPA Chapter 1, 3 and 4

Week 2   Computer system engineering
Hardware and software issues
Allocation
Readings: SEPA Chapter 5

Week 3   Project planning and organization
Software cost and schedule estimation techniques
Cost models
Risk analysis Project Abstract due
Readings: SEPA Chapter 6

Week 4   Analysis fundamentals
Object-oriented analysis
Introduction to data flow techniques
Readings: SEPA Chapter 7 and 8

Week 5   Creating Flow Models
Data flow representations
Control flow representations or OOA techniques
Data modeling
A specification approach
Project Plan due
Readings: SEPA Chapters 9 (9.6 and 9.7), Chapter 10

Week 6   Elements of software design
Fundamental concepts
Architectural, Data and Procedural Design
Design representation methods

Week 7   Mid term exam
Requirements specification due
Readings: SEPA Chapters 11 and 12

Week 8   Data flow oriented design
Data structure oriented design
Examples and exercises
Preliminary design due
Readings: Chapters 14 (if desired) and 15 (if desired)

Week 9   Elements of Real-time design
Object-oriented design and programming
Examples and exercises
Readings: SEPA Chapters 16 (if desired) and 17

Week 10   Programming languages
Coding style and clarity
Software Quality Assurance and reliability
Detail design due
Readings: SEPA Chapters 18 and 19

Week 11   White-box testing methods
Black-box testing methods
Example and exercises
Readings: SEPA Chapters 20 (portions only) and 21

Week 12   Testing Strategies
Debugging
Test Specification due
Readings: SEPA Chapter 22

Week 13   Software Maintenance
Software Configuration Management
CASE

Week 14   Project presentations
All remaining documentation, source listing due

A 2.5 hour final exam is given as part of the course described above. Homework is suggested, but not graded [if I had a grad assistant (I didn't), it would have been graded].

The major challenge in any software engineering course is coordination of lecture material with knowledge required to complete project deliverable. Colleagues at other institutions have gone so far as to require that the entire SEPA text be read within the first month of the course (a bit much, I think) so that students will have been introduced to all necessary techniques and methods.

4.2.2 A Software Engineering Course that Emphasizes Methods

A course of this type emphasizes methods to the exclusion of other important aspects of the discipline. I would strongly recommend that you assign readings in other areas (e.g., SQA, maintenance, SCM) even if you do not cover these topics in lecture. It's not a bad idea to test on these topics and to grade adequacy in methods using the course project.

Week 1 The impact of software
     The software crisis and the "aging software plant"
     An overview of software engineering
     Discussion of project requirements and topics
     Computer system engineering
     Readings: SEPA Chapters 1 and 5

Week 2 Analysis fundamentals
     FAST
     Creating Flow Models
     Data flow representations
     Readings: SEPA Chapters 6 and 7

Week 3 Control flow representations
     Data structure representation
     A specification approach
     Project description due
     Readings: SEPA Chapter 8

Week 4 Object-oriented analysis
     Data modeling
     Software requirements specification due
     Readings: SEPA Chapter 9

Week 5 Alternative analysis methods
     Formal methods for specification
     Readings SEPA Chapter 10

Week 6 Elements of software design
     Fundamental concepts
     Architectural, Data and Procedural Design

Design representation methods

Week 7   Mid term exam
         Readings: SEPA Chapters 11 and 12

Week 8   Data flow oriented design
         Data structure oriented design
         Examples and exercises
         Preliminary design due
         Readings: SEPA Chapters 14 and 15

Week 9   Object-oriented design
         Interface design
         Readings: SEPA Chapters 18 and 19

Week 10   Elements of real-time design
         Examples and exercises
         Readings: Chapters 22 and 23

Week 11   White-box testing methods
         Black-box testing methods
         Example and exercises

Week 12   Testing Strategies
         Debugging
         Test Specification due

Week 13   Project Presentations

Week 14   Project presentations
         All remaining documentation, source listing due

A 2.5 hour final exam is given as part of the course described above. Homework is probably not in order because of time pressure. However, selected problems may be assigned to emphasize important points.

4.2.3 An Analysis-Oriented Course

The primary focus of this course is to cover analysis methods within the context of the software engineering process. A term project is assigned, but the deliverable is a complete software requirements specification and or prototypes that is considerably more detailed (and hopefully, higher quality) than those required in the course already described. A course of this type emphasizes analysis to the exclusion of other important aspects of the discipline. I would strongly recommend that you assign readings in other areas, even if you do not cover other topics in lecture.

SEPA is adequate as the only textbook for an undergraduate course of this type. However, a graduate offering should supplement SEPA with other readings from books dedicated to the subject of analysis. See Appendix I for suggestions.

Week 1   The impact of software
           The software crisis and the "aging software plant"
           An overview of software engineering
           Discussion of project requirements and topics
           Readings: SEPA Chapters 1 and 5

Week 2   Computer System Engineering
           Readings: SEPA Chapter 6

Week 3   Analysis fundamentals
           FAST
           Project description due
           An overview of the methods
           Readings: SEPA Chapter 7

Week 4   Creating Flow Models
           Data flow representations
           Data dictionary
           Examples and exercises

Week 5   Control flow representations
           Data structure representation
           A specification approach

Week 6   Presentation of analysis models (if SA is used)
           Readings: SEPA Chapter 8

Week 7   Mid-Term exam

Week 8   Object-oriented analysis

Data modeling
Readings: SEPA Chapter 9

Week 9   Presentation of analysis models (if OOA is used)

Week 10   Alternative analysis methods
          JSD—an overview
          DSSD—an overview
          Other methods (chosen by the instructor)

Week 11   Formal methods for specification
          Examples and exercises

Week 12   Software requirements specification due
          Presentations
          Readings: SEPA Chapters 10, 11, and 12

Week 13
Presentation focuses on the relationship of the topics to requirements analysis, modeling and specification.
          Elements of software design and testing
          Structured design—an overview
          OOD—an overview
          Readings: SEPA Chapters 17 and 19

Week 14
Presentation focuses on the relationship of the topics to requirements analysis, modeling and specification.
          SQA—an overview
          Testing—an overview

A 2.5 hour final exam is given as part of the course described above. Homework can be assigned to emphasize important points.

4.2.4 A Design-Oriented Course

The primary focus of this course is to cover design methods within the context of the software engineering process. A term project is assigned, but the deliverable is a complete software requirements and design specification that is considerably more detailed (and hopefully, higher quality) than those required in the courses 4.2.1 and 4.2.2. A course of this type emphasizes design (and to some extent analysis) to the exclusion of other important aspects of the discipline. I would strongly recommend that you assign readings in other areas, even if you do not cover other topics in lecture.

SEPA is adequate as the only textbook for an undergraduate course of this type. However, a graduate offering should supplement SEPA with other readings from books dedicated to the subject of design. See Appendix I for suggestions.

Week 1	The impact of software
	The software crisis and the "aging software plant"
	An overview of software engineering
	Computer System Engineering
	Discussion of project requirements and topics
	Readings: SEPA Chapters 1, 5, and 6
Week 2	Analysis fundamentals
	Creating Flow Models
	Data flow representations
	Data dictionary
	Project description due
	Readings: SEPA Chapter 7 and 8
Week 3	Control flow representations
	Data structure representation
	A specification approach
	Requirements models due
Week 4	Object-oriented analysis
	Data modeling
	Readings: SEPA Chapter 10
Week 5	Elements of software design
	Fundamental concepts
	Architectural, Data and Procedural Design
	Design representation methods
Week 6	Mid term exam
	Readings: SEPA Chapters 11

Week 7   Data flow oriented design
            Data structure oriented design
            Examples and exercises
            Preliminary design due
            Readings: SEPA Chapters 12

Week 8   Object-oriented design
            Readings: SEPA Chapters 13

Week 9   Alternative Design methods
            DSSD—an overview
            JSD—an overview
            Other methods that instructor introduced
            Readings: SEPA Chapters 14

Week 10   Interface design
            Draft detail design due
            Readings: SEPA Chapter 15

Week 11   Elements of real-time design
            Examples and exercises
            Readings: SEPA Chapter 17 and 18

Week 12
Presentation focuses on the relationship of the topics to design.
            SQA—an overview
            Testing—an overview
            Test case design
            Readings: SEPA Chapter 22 and 23

Week 13
Presentation focuses on the relationship of the topics to design.
            CASE tools
            The CASE repository
            Integration issues

Week 14   Design documentation due
            Presentations

A 2.5 hour final exam is given as part of the course described above. Homework can be assigned to emphasize important points.

4.2.5 A Management-Oriented Course

Courses of this type are more likely to be offered in information systems or business programs that have a software engineering focus. Although I believe a course such as this would be important in a computer-science or computer engineering curriculum, the realities of an already overloaded curriculum preclude this.

The primary focus of this course is to cover management methods within the context of the software engineering process. A term project is assigned, but the deliverable is a project plan that is considerably more detailed (and hopefully, higher quality) than those required in the courses 4.2.1 and 4.2.2. A course of this type emphasizes design (and to some extent analysis) to the exclusion of other important aspects of the discipline. I would strongly recommend that you assign readings in other areas, even if you do not cover other topics in lecture.

Ideally, much of the project planning work that is part of the term project should be performed using one or more CASE tools.

SEPA is adequate as the only textbook for an undergraduate course of this type. However, a graduate offering should supplement SEPA with other readings from books dedicated to the subject of design. See Appendix I for suggestions.

Week 1   The impact of software
         The software crisis and the "aging software plant"
         An overview of software engineering
         Readings: SEPA Chapter 1

Week 2   Software Engineering Methods
         System Engineering
         Requirements Analysis
         Readings: selections sections from
         SEPA Chapters 5, 6, 7, and 8

Week 3   Software Engineering Methods
         Software design
         Software testing
         Umbrella activities
         Readings: selections sections from

SEPA Chapters 10, 11, 12, 14, 16, 19

Week 4   Software metrics
Management metrics
LOC and function point normalization
Technical metrics—an overview
Readings: SEPA Chapter 2 and 3

Week 5   Project planning
Estimation techniques
Examples and exercises
Readings: SEPA Chapter 4

Week 6   Risk analysis
Identification
Projection
Management and monitoring
Readings: outside readings
(see **Further Readings** in SEPA Chapter 4)

Week 7:   Project planning
Scheduling
Task networks and resource allocation
Acquisition

Week 8   Mid term exam
Readings: SEPA Chapter 17

Week 9   Software quality assurance
Statistical SQA
Formal technical reviews
SQA management
Readings: SEPA Chapter 20

Week 10   Software maintenance
Issues and costs
Management of the process
Reverse and re-engineering
Readings: SEPA Chapter 21

Week 11   Software configuration management
Change and related management issues

SCM tasks
The impact of the project database
Readings: selected sections from
SEPA Chapters 22 and 23

Week 12 CASE
The choice of tools
Integration issues

Week 13, 14 Management presentations
Project Plan due

5 GUIDELINES FOR SHORT COURSES & SEMINARS

Over the past 15 years, I have had the opportunity to conduct short courses and seminars in software engineering that have been attended by over 20,000 software practitioners and managers. To be effective, a short course in software engineering must have the following attributes:

Focus. The course tone and presentation must be tuned to the audience; i.e., a course for managers must stress different topics than a course for technical practitioners.
Practicality. Although it is important to note research directions and assess their long term impact, most short course participants are interested in practical tools and techniques that are viable now.
Content. All phases of the software engineering process should be presented, even if different emphasis is applied for different audiences.
Problem solving. Students should participate in "laboratory sessions" in which limited problem solving is used to reinforce concepts introduced during lectures.
Supplementary materials. One or more books (e.g. SEPA) should be used to reinforce course materials and provide depth that is otherwise impossible to include in a 3, 4 or 5 day short course.

Many universities and private organizations sponsor two to five day public seminars/courses in software engineering and related topics. In fact, this can be an extremely effective way for your department to establish better ties to local industry and to raise (what can amount to) substantial revenue for yourself and your department or institution. Many larger institutions direct market their short courses on a national basis.

SEPA can provide a foundation for software engineering training that can be tailored to specific market requirements and application areas.

When software engineering discipline taught in an industry short course setting, three specific audiences can be addressed:

1. business managers
2. technical managers
3. technical practitioners

Business managers should be introduced to software engineering and to the importance of software as a critical system element for the 1990s. Their decisions will affect the manner in which software development methods are applied within a company. Technical managers (and their counterparts in other engineering and customer organizations) must understand how to plan and control software development. Technical practitioners must be provided with a suite of methods and tools that may be applied during the definition, development and maintenance phases.

On the pages that follow, I have included outlines for a number of courses that are appropriate for one or more of the constituencies noted above. Each of these courses is offered by R.S. Pressman & Associates, Inc. and is supported by extensive courseware. Each is supplemented with SEPA. If you have an interest in establishing a short course program at your institution, contact RSP&A at (203) 795-5044 or FAX: (203) 799-1023 for further information. The course descriptions include a general statement of objectives and a content outline.

A SHORT COURSE: MANAGING SOFTWARE PROJECTS

Audience: Managers and senior technical staff who must plan, control and track software development projects.

Duration: 2-3 days

Abstract: This course introduces modern software project management practices in the context of software engineering technology. Effective paradigms for software engineering are introduced; an brief overview of modern software engineering techniques is provided; risk management techniques are discussed; estimation and scheduling methods are considered; and tracking and control mechanisms are presented; management aspects of software quality assurance and software configuration management are described. In addition, the planning and management of software projects that make use of CASE tools is considered.

Questions to be answered:

- What are the key challenges for software project managers?
- What is the current state of software engineering practice in the industry?
- How do I develop a meaningful effort and time estimates?
- How do I assess risk at the beginning of a project?
- What can I do to manage and reduce risk?
- What tools are available to help me manage?
- How can I control my projects more effectively?
- How will a software quality assurance program help?
- Is there a way to control and monitor change?
- How do I track project status?
- How do I implement these new technologies?

Outline:

Software Project Management
    The nature of software projects
    Why projects fail?
    Basic elements of project management
        Project planning
        Project control
        Project tracking
Software Engineering: Management Overview
    The elements of the technology

Paradigms for software engineering
    The changing life cycle
    Using prototypes
    The spiral model
    Automation based approaches
Methods
    Analysis, Design, Coding and Testing
    Maintenance and re-engineering
CASE

Software Project Planning
How does the process begin
The nature of estimation
Using historical data
    collecting software metrics
    metrics—uses and limitations
Cost/effort estimation
    The impact of software metrics
    Conventional methods
    Empirical models
Risk management
    Risk assessment
        identification
        analysis
        prioritization
    Risk control
    Documenting and managing risk
Creating a project schedule
    Work breakdown structure
    Interdependency
    Establishing milestones
    Using CPM and related tools
    Updating the schedule
Organizing people for the project
    One person projects
    Small teams
    Large projects
        An organizational architecture
        The lines of communication
Creating a project plan
    A typical plan
    Reviewing the plan

Software Project Control
Answering the question "Where are we?"
Controlling progress
    Managing to the schedule

Isolating problem areas
"Re-routing" the project
Controlling Quality—Software Quality Assurance
The elements of SQA
Using formal technical reviews
Statistical SQA
Controlling Quality—Software Configuration Management
SCM functions
The necessity for change control
Software Project Tracking
Conventional tracking mechanisms
The daily/weekly/monthly progress report
Micro-milestones
Holding Successful meetings
Recognizing when to revise (schedule, budget, expectations)
Implementing Software Engineering & CASE
The technology should be there before you start
The Implementation Life Cycle

A SHORT COURSE: SOFTWARE ENGINEERING METHODS

Audience: Managers technical staff who must understand the modern software engineering methods and how to apply them.

Duration: 2-4 days

Abstract: This course introduces modern software engineering methods. Paradigms for software development are emphasized. The bridge between the customer and the system is described. Analysis methods, with an emphasis on structured analysis, are presented. Design fundamentals and methods are described. Coding and languages are discussed, and testing methods and strategies are presented. The impact of CASE tools across all methods is described.

Questions to be answered:

• How are software engineering paradigms applied on real projects?
• What techniques can be used to help the developer and customer define requirements?
• What are the notation, the tools, and the approach used for

structured analysis?
- What are the fundamental "measures" of design quality?
- How do I move from an analysis model to a design model?
- How can I used structured design? what is object-oriented design?
- How do languages impact the process?
- Is there a strategy and tactics for software testing? What is "test case design?"
- What CASE tools are available to help me?

Outline:

Software Engineering
    The elements of the technology
    Paradigms for software engineering
    Methods
    CASE

Facilitated Application Specification Techniques
    Working with the customer—FAST
    The FAST meeting
    Developing a Functional Specification

Requirements Analysis and Specification
    System engineering and allocation
    Analysis principles
    Bounding and the statement of scope
    Defining objects and operations
    What if the customer is unsure?
    An overview of analysis methods

Structured Analysis
    Creating the flow model
    Control and process specifications
    The requirements (data) dictionary
    The impact of CASE
    Data modeling—an overview
    Defining system architecture
    Specification Principles

Software Design
    Design Fundamentals
    Data design—an overview
    Architectural design
    Mapping techniques for structured design
    Procedural design

Interface design—an overview
Object-oriented design—an overview
Languages and Coding
Programming language fundamentals
Language generations and their impact
Coding style
Software Testing
Basic objectives
Test case design
White-box methods
Black-box methods
Testing strategies
Debugging
CASE: Technical Issues
What is CASE—really?
Data, interface and tools integration
Environments and related issues
Course Wrap-up

A SHORT COURSE: SOFTWARE MEASUREMENT & METRICS

Audience: Technical managers and staff who must understand process and product metrics, how to collect them and how to use them to improve software quality.

Duration: 2 days

Abstract: This course considers both process and product metrics that are useful in the management of software projects and the evaluation of the product that is produced. The collection, calculation and evaluation of pragmatic metrics is emphasized. Laboratory sessions are used to reinforce important concepts.

Outline:

Metrics and Software Engineering
Why is measurement important?
What is the controversy?
An emphasis on quality
Process Metrics

Hard data
Soft data
How it should be collected
Normalization
The options
Size-oriented metrics
Function oriented metrics
Selecting the appropriate approach
Function Point Metrics
The benefits
Calculating FP
Extensions for Feature Points
Backfiring
Typical industry data
Building a Process Model
Collection
Computation
Evaluation
Using Process Metrics
Project estimation
Tools justification
Process assessment
Project Estimation
Metrics-based estimation techniques
Cost and effort
Quality
Tools Justification
Calculating ROI
Process Assessment
How metrics are used to improve quality
Statistical quality assurance
The Pareto Principle
Isolating the vital few
Product Metrics
Measuring the technical quality of design
IEEE Std. 982.2-1988 Measures
Design Metrics
Architectural metrics
Traceability and compliance
Cyclomatic complexity
Halstead's metrics
Other design metrics

> **Testing and Operational Metrics**
>> Fault density and failure profiles
>> Software maturity index
>> Reliability
> **Establishing a Metrics Program**
>> An implementation strategy
>> Creating guidelines
>> Selling the concept
>> Uses and abuses of metrics
>> The need for education
> **Course Wrap-up**

SEMINAR: THE CHALLENGE OF SOFTWARE DEVELOPMENT

Audience: Business managers with an interest in software development; managers with direct and indirect responsibility for software development and maintenance; technical staff who require an overview of software engineering issues

Duration: 3 -4 hours

Description: This seminar discusses software as a strategy business issue, software engineering as an enabling technology, CASE, and guidelines for making the technology work within a company that adopts it.

Learning Objectives:
• to understand the nature of computer software and the software engineering process and why it requires management attention
• to view CASE as a tool set that forms an environment for software development
• to understand the impact of software engineering and CASE on productivity and quality
• to outline a strategy for instituting the technology

Outline:

> **What is software and why is it important?**
>> defining software
>> management challenges
> **Measurement and software engineering**
>> why measurement leads to good management

> what do we measure?
> how do we measure it?
> what do we do with the measures?
> **The challenge of change**
> **Software engineering & CASE—a management view**
> **Managing the transition to SE/CASE**
> the implementation life cycle—an overview
> assessment
> education
> selection
> installation
> evaluation

SEMINAR: CASE: A TECHNOLOGY OVERVIEW

Audience: Managers with direct and indirect responsibility for software development and maintenance; technical staff who require an overview of CASE and related software engineering issues; other staff members who want to understand CASE

Duration: 2-3 hours

Description: This seminar describes the basic technological components of computer-aided software engineering (CASE). The underlying software engineering technology is described; a taxonomy of tools is defined; each tool category is described; integration issues are discussed, and trends are identified.

Learning Objectives:
• to understand how the components of software engineering interrelate with CASE
• to appreciate key management and technical issues that affect CASE
• to learn what tool types are available and to describe each tool category
• to understand the basic issues and elements of an integrated project support environment (IPSE)
• to be cognizant of future trends in CASE

Outline:
> **Defining a context for CASE**
> **The underlying technology**
> software engineering
> methods overview

procedures overview
CASE
historical perspective
Why CASE today?
Management issues
Technical issues
Tool categories
needs and focus (for each tool category)
representative function (for each category)
The elements of an IPSE
the CASE repository
the common interface
the software backplane
CASE standards and their impact
Where is CASE headed?

SEMINAR: MAKING SOFTWARE ENGINEERING HAPPEN

Audience: Senior managers with responsibility for managing technological change; managers with direct and indirect responsibility for software development and maintenance; technical staff who will be "agents of change" within their software development organization

Duration 3 - hours

Description: This seminar describes a five step approach for instituting software engineering methods, procedures and tools within an organization. Basic technology transfer issues are discussed; technology assessment techniques are described, education strategies are presented; methods and tools (CASE) selection criteria and guidelines are discussed, installation and evaluation strategies are described.

Learning Objectives:
• to understand the issues associated with technology transfer
• to formulate an effective strategy for instituting CASE and software engineering practices
• to learn how to assess an organization using both quantitative and qualitative techniques
• to appreciate the need for a software engineering education
• to establish viable criteria for CASE tools selection
• to understand how to properly install CASE tools and software engineering methods
• to understand how to evaluate what you've done

Outline:

Why do we struggle with technology implementation?
management issues
technical issues
cultural issues

The implementation life cycle
navigating the maze
the benefits of a systematic approach

Assessment
conducting the audit
the SEI approach
the Pressman approach
quantitative and qualitative findings
preparing an assessment report

Education
why is it important
a self assessment test
options and recommendations

Selection
general guidelines
establishing criteria
key issues for CASE

Installation
tasks
milestones and deliverables
assigning responsibility
overall guidelines

Evaluation
metrics
staff debriefing

Summary

6

CHAPTER GUIDELINES

Software Engineering: A Practitioner's Approach (SEPA) has been organized into five parts that address the primary concerns of most practicing software engineers and the topic focus of most professors who teach the subject. In this segment of the Instructor's Manual, guidelines for the use of each of the chapters in SEPA are presented.

The chapters in Part I of the book focus on defining the technology, describing software engineering paradigms, introducing the importance of measurement and metrics, and establishing a basis for project planning and management. Chapters in Part II of the book present the fundamental concepts and specific methods that are used to analyze systems and software and specify requirements that are derived as a consequence of analysis. The chapters of Past III focus on design and implementation, moving from fundamental concepts through a number of important design methods and culminating with a discussion of languages and coding. Part IV is dedicated to the activities that are required to ensure quality and manage change. Chapters focus on SQA, testing, maintenance and configuration management. Finally, Part V presents a view of automation, considering CASE and development environments as well as a look into the future.

6.1 AN ABBREVIATED JOURNEY THROUGH THE BOOK

Before presenting a more detailed discussion of each chapter, I though it might be worthwhile to provide you with a thumbnail sketch of the book.

Part I—Software, the Process and its Management

Chapter 1 introduces software and software engineering and is mandatory reading for all introductory courses (and many advanced presentations as well). The course describes three primary components of software (programs, documents and data) and three primary components of software engineering (procedures, methods and tools).

Chapter 2 focuses on the importance of measurement and metrics. Both quality and productivity metrics are emphasized, with primary emphasis being placed on LOC and function point measures. This sets the stage for their use in project planning.

Chapter 3 focuses on project planning, presenting important techniques for cost and effort estimation. Decomposition and empirical models for cost estimation are considered.

Chapter 4 continues the discussion of project planning, but here I emphasize risk analysis, scheduling and acquisition related issues. Organizational approaches and the content *Project Plan* are also considered.

Part II—System and Software Requirements Analysis

Throughout SEPA, software is viewed in a system context; that is, software is presented as one element of a computer-based system that must interface with other elements such as hardware, people, data bases, etc. Chapter 5 introduces the basic principles of computer-based system engineering and provides the reader with the answer to the question: "Where do requirements for software come from?"

Chapter 6 presents the fundamental principles of all analysis activities, emphasizing analysis of the information domain. The content of the *Software Requirements Specification* is also presented.

Chapter 7 introduces the notation, heuristics and modeling approach that is called structured analysis. Both conventional and real-time software modeling is considered.

Chapter 8 presents the basic concepts and modeling notation for object-oriented analysis. In addition, data modeling notation and the entity relationship diagram are introduced.

Chapter 9 considers DSSD and JSD as alternative analysis methods. More importantly, the chapter introduced the notation and approach for formal specification, using the Z Specification language as an example.

Part III—The Design and Implementation of Software

Chapter 10 introduces a set of basic design concepts that may be used as an indicator of software quality. The concepts of data, architectural, procedural and interface design are introduced, and the content of the *Design Specification* is presented.

Chapter 11 presents the notation, heuristics and mapping approach that is called structured design (this chapter is coupled with Chapter 7) . The concept of program architecture (structure) is introduced and methods for assessing structural quality are considered.

Chapter 12 presents concepts and notation that can be used to perform object-oriented design (this chapter is coupled with Chapter 8). Booch's notation for design modeling is introduced.

Chapter 13 presents an overview of the approach and notation that is used to perform DSSD and JSD design steps (this chapter is coupled with Chapter 9).

Chapter 14 introduces the concepts that should be understood to design effective human-computer interfaces. Human factors are considered briefly and specific guidelines for interface design are presented.

Chapter 15 presents a reasonably thorough discussion of software design for real-time systems, beginning with an overview of key design criteria for real-time software and then moving into a discussion of specific design methodology and notation.

Chapter 16 discusses programming languages in the context of software engineering. Language classes are suggested, the basic attributes of a "good" programming language are proposed and the elements of good programming style are presented.

Part IV—Ensuring, Verifying and Maintaining Software Integrity

Chapter 17 focuses on software quality assurance (SQA) with specific emphasis on formal technical reviews. The basic factors that influence software quality are surveyed, the elements of an SQA approach are defined and the manner in which reviews are conducted is presented in detail.

Chapters 18 and 19 present the fundamental objective, overall strategy and specific methodology associated with software testing. Chapter 18 considers the basic objectives of testing and presents a series of white-box and black-box testing techniques. Chapter 19 focuses on testing strategy and also discusses the elements of software debugging.

Chapter 20 discusses software maintenance. Procedural aspects of the maintenance activity are considered and reverse and re-engineering methods are discussed.

Chapter 21 presents a technical discussion of SCM. The four primary activities associated with this important software engineering "umbrella" activity are presented and the concept of configuration objects and the project database (the repository) are introduced.

Part V—The Role of Automation

Chapter 22 discusses computer-aided software engineering and presents a taxonomy of CASE tools. The categorization of tools is done functionally and is complemented by reference to representative tools in the **Further Readings** section of the chapter.

Chapter 23 consider integrated CASE environments, with specific emphasis on integration options, the architecture required to develop a software engineering environment, tools integration issues and the CASE repository.

Chapter 24 takes a look at the road ahead for software engineering. The chapters argues that the three components of the technology—procedures, methods and tools will each evolve in predictable ways as we approach the millennium year.

Each SEPA chapter is discussed in the pages that follow. Each discussion begins with an indication of the overall intent of the chapter and a critical concept that should be emphasized. A general overview of the chapter is presented with suggestions for supplementary topics for lecture presentation or assignments. Finally, Problems and Points to Ponder are discussed.

It is important to note that Part V of this guide is not a "solution manual" to Problems and Points to Ponder. Many of the "problems" have no unique solution. Rather, I have attempted to comment on some of the problems and to assist in an analysis of input from your students.

Part I

Chapter 1
Software and
Software Engineering

INTENT

The intent of this chapter is to introduce the true nature of computer software and the engineering approach that can be applied to create higher quality software. The chapter describes a set of important characteristics that are associated with all software, identifies the historical reasons for the problems that we often encounter, and introduces the paradigms that are commonly applied for software engineering.

Critical Points: Software is one element of a computer based system. The early days of programming were relatively undisciplined, leading to a set of problems that continue to plague modern software development. Software engineering is a disciplined approach to software development.

CHAPTER OVERVIEW AND COMMENTS

Sections 1.1 and 1.2 present software using an historical perspective. A textbook definition of "software" is juxtaposed with a discussion of characteristics that more completely describe the true nature of software. Basic "components" of software are described and important software application areas are delineated. This section may seem "old hat" to some readers; however, it is intended to level different degrees of experience and historical knowledge among the students.

Section 1.3 describes the problems that have lead to a "software crisis." To help emphasize the impact of poor quality software, it might be worthwhile to discuss a few "software horror stories" during lecture. Such real life examples (some quite humorous) will have far greater impact than an abstract discussion. *ACM Software Engineering Notes* and more recently the *CACM* (last page) publishes Peter Neumann's Risks to the Public. (Note: An index of these risks was published in the SEN, vol. 16, no. 1, January, 1991, p. 2ff). This is a gold mine of horror stories from every conceivable application area.

Section 1.4 presents a set of myths that are still believed by more than a few practitioners and managers. Indirectly, these myths can help you to further depict the characteristics of software and the manner in which it is developed.

Section 1.5—one of the most important sections in SEPA— describes each of the major software engineering paradigms. Because the concepts introduced here will be referenced repeatedly through the book, it is extremely important to dedicate adequate lecture time to them. An IEEE Tutorial, *New Paradigms for Software Development* (W.W. Agresti, 1986) will provide a rich assortment of important papers that can be used to supplement SEPA.

Section 1.6 defines the generic phases of the software engineering process—definition, development and maintenance. Like the preceding section, ideas introduced here are critically important. Adequate lecture time should be allocated to be certain that students understand the purpose of each phase.

PROBLEMS AND POINTS TO PONDER

1.1 Classic examples include the use of "digital automobile dashboards" to impart a high tech, high quality image. Appliances that "think;" the broad array of consumer electronics; personal computers (today, differentiated more by their software function than the hardware), industrial instrumentation and machines.

1.2 The apprentice/artist culture of the 1950s and 1960s worked fine for single person, well constrained projects. Today, applications are more complex, teams work on large projects, and software outlives generations of developers. Yet, the culture established in the early days dies hard, leading more than a little resistance to more disciplined methods.

1.3 This is a good problem for classroom discussion (time permitting). Rather than focusing on cliche' ridden (albeit important) issues of privacy, quality of life, etc., you might want to discuss "technofright" and how software can help to exacerbate or remedy it. Another interesting possibility is to use

Neumann's "Risks" column in SEN to key discussion.

1.5   Another way to characterize this problem is to suggest that each student describe a software myth that he or she believed that has subsequently been dispelled. From the student's point of view, myths will likely be driven by programming projects that they've attempted earlier in their career.

1.6   I strongly recommend that you assign this problem now and near the end of the course. You'll be able to use the CASE tools available to you as part of the Software Engineering Teaching System (see Segment 2) as demos. You can initiate a "request for information campaign," having your student write to vendors and build a library of information on CASE for later analysis.

1.7   Assign this problem as is if the majority of your class is composed of industry practitioners. If your students are "green," suggest a project scenario and ask the students to identify the appropriate paradigm.

1.8   Software applications that are relatively easy to prototype almost always involve human-machine interaction and/or heavy computer graphics. Other applications that are sometimes amenable to prototyping are certain classes of mathematical algorithms, subset of command driven systems and other applications where results can be easily examined without real-time interaction. Applications that are difficult to prototype include control and process control functions, many classes of real-time applications and embedded software.

1.10 Ideally, your students should have the opportunity to use a 4GL at some point during the course, if for no other reason than to appreciate its strengths and weaknesses. See comments for Problem 1.6. You might take a similar approach here.

1.11 Taking a classical hardware-oriented view of maintenance, adaptive and perfective maintenance applied to software should not really be called maintenance at all. Both are development activities. Historically, however, we have termed these activities maintenance. However, the terminology can be very important if it is misunderstood by management or leads to bad allocation of resources.

1.12 The maintenance phase is generally not encountered for embedded software. In most cases, embedded software is defined and developed, but once it is placed in its host environment, it is not likely to change. Note: be sure to emphasize that this is not always the case, e.g., in products that are updated, in situations in which advanced versions of a product are created.

Chapter 2
Project Management:
Software Metrics

INTENT

The intent of this chapter is to introduce the importance of measurement and metrics. The chapter begins with an overview of the entire project management process, thereby setting the stage for Chapters 3 and 4. Then, the role of productivity and quality measurement is emphasized and the use of these measures in project planning activities is foreshadowed. Both LOC and function point normalized metrics are considered.

Critical Points: Measurement is an important part of software project management. There is no universal agreement on the best measures, but most use either size (LOC) or function (function point) as the normalizing factor. Metrics for quality are as important (if not more so, that those for productivity (see Chapter 17 for more on this.

CHAPTER OVERVIEW AND COMMENTS

Section 2.1 presents an overview of the project management process. Even if you don't intend to assign Chapters 3 and 4, you should assign this section as reading and discuss it briefly in class.

Section 2.2 and 2.3 present the spectrum of measurement that is used in software engineering and introduced both size-oriented and function-oriented measures. You should emphasize the anomalies that can occur when size oriented measures are used. For detail on this, see Capers Jones' new book (in preparation at the time of this writing) published by McGraw-Hill. If you decide to use FP as your metric, see Dreger's book on the subject. It contains lots of practical guidance for FP use.

Section 2.4 introduces quality metrics and should be supplemented by reading in Chapter 17 if you intend to go into the subject in detail at this time.

Section 2.5 provide guidance for "peaceful coexistence" among different metrics approaches (no easy matter in the real world!) Be careful how you discuss the backfiring technique. It is controversial and implies a direct connection between LOC and FP which must be tempered by common sense. The factors noted by Zelkowitz and Basili should be emphasized to convince students that one-to-one comparisons of different software engineering groups probably make little sense.

Section 2.6 can be omitted if you're teaching an under-graduate course. It discusses pragmatic issues that are critically important to industry people but can be skipped at the under-graduate level.

PROBLEMS AND POINTS TO PONDER

2.1 This is the first appearance of the *SafeHome* system that will recur throughout the book. Even if you normally don't assign homework, you might try this one. What you're looking for is a reasonable work breakdown structure, but you students will struggle because they don't have a bounded scope. You can help them by defining the basic characteristics of *SafeHome* (see later chapters, use the SEPA index for pointers to the problem).

2.2 Direct metrics:
1. number of pages
2. number of figures
3. number of distinct documents

Indirect measures:
1. readability (use the FOG index)
2. completeness (count the number of "help desk" questions that you receive)
3. maintainability (time to make a documentation change)

2.3 Two people, A and B, develop the same program. Each does a good job, satisfies all requirements and takes exactly one week to complete the job.. A uses 100 LOC, B does the job with 50 LOC. Is A twice as productive as B?

When large numbers of projects are considered, an averaging affect tends to mitigate the problem implied above.

2.4 Use the templates contained in Figures 2.3 and 2.4. See

Dreger for guidelines on counting number of ... values. They are given in this problem, but are not always obvious in real problems.

2.7   Refer to Chapter 14 and related references for appropriate definitions.

2.8   Yes. Although the error count can go down, the error remaining can be difficult and cost significantly more than avarage. Since spoilage is a cost measure, it can increase even if the instantaneous defects/LOC decreases.

2.9   No. The level of abstraction of most 4GLs is too high.

2.12 This has been done and is presented in Grady and Caswell [GRA87].

Chapter **3**
Project Management:
Estimation

INTENT

The intent of this chapter is to introduce concrete guidelines for software project planning with specific emphasis on estimation. Issues and techniques associated with software cost, duration, and effort estimation are described in detail. The use of software metrics as a "baseline" for estimation is also emphasized. Upon completing this chapter, the student should understand how to develop a cost estimate for a software project.

Critical Points: Software cost can be systematically estimated if historical data are available. Accurate estimation requires a decomposition of project tasks and/or software functions. Empirical models and automated tools can assist the planner.

CHAPTER OVERVIEW AND COMMENTS

The issues that are associated with software project planning span a broad range of topics that include project estimation techniques, management considerations and an early assessment of scope of effort and resources to be applied. It is important to emphasize that good planning does take experience and that neophyte planners generally tend to be overly optimistic. Remind students of Murphy's law and all corollaries.

Sections 3.1 and 3.2 describe a basic software planning philosophy that recognizes the "danger" of estimation, while at the same time emphasizing the necessity of estimation. You should discuss and expand upon the implications of Figure 3.1 (especially in a university course where little real life experience among students is the norm).

Section 3.3 describes the need for a well-bounded software scope. You should provide a number of examples of ambiguous, unbounded statements of scope, e.g., "The XYZ system will read a number of input ports in real-time, selecting appropriate input for processing and transmitting control signals to one or more distributed process controllers." Have your students critique this scope, suggesting areas of ambiguity and points of clarification. You might play the customer of the XYZ system answering questions as they are posed by students. Among the key questions should be:

- how many input ports?
- what characterizes "input"?
- what performance bounds may be used to define real-time?
- how is "appropriate" input selected?
- what kind of processing?
- define transmitted
  - what media, what protocol, what distance, what mechanism?
- describe "control signals"

and so on. Based on answers to these and other questions, have student teams develop a well-defined scope. Also, be sure that student understand the use of *decomposition* in the context of project planning.

Section 3.4 discusses resources that are essential for a successful software development effort. A discussion on software tools and CASE might be appropriate at this point. Additionally, descriptions of modern programming environments such as Smalltalk, InterLisp, Ada, etc. might be worthwhile here. However, don't let the students infer that human resources are less important, when in fact they provide the greatest challenge for the software project manager. The brief overview of CASE tools presented here is a prelude to Chapters 22 and 23. In a management oriented course (see segment 4 of this *Instructor's Manual*), it might be worthwhile to assign more readings out of Chapter 22 at this time. The discussion of reusability is brief, but it is very important! You might want to expand on the SEPA presentation with supplementary materials of your own. See [TRA88] for guidance. The discussion of reusability recurs at a number of points throughout the book.

Section 3.5 is a somewhat philosophical discussion of project estimation. Be sure to cover the four points noted on page 75 (SEPA) during lecture.

Sections 3.6 through 3.8 discuss software cost and effort estimation techniques in considerable detail. The material in these sections is generally sufficient for most software engineering courses. However, if you feel that supplementary material is required, books by Arthur, Boehm, Jones, Putnam and others noted in Appendix I are excellent sources of information.

PROBLEMS AND POINTS TO PONDER

3.1 Sometimes, complexity arises from a poorly established interface between the customer and the software developer. Discounting that, the following technical characteristics should be considered:

> real-time attributes
> multiprocessing requirement
> (concurrency)
> nature of the algorithm
> requirement for recursion
> nature of input
> determinacy of input
> nature of output
> language characteristics

. . . and knowledge/experience of staff on application.

3.2 Use the approach described in the discussion of section 3.3 to structure the critique of student presentations. Be on the lookout for ambiguity. An interesting way to "grade" this problem is to have a team of students review each other's scope to point out problems.

3.3 Performance:
- real time application—raw processing of data measured by CPU time and possibly interrupt servicing efficiency
- engineering/scientific applications—numerical accuracy and for large systems, CPU time.
- commercial applications—I/O efficiency
- interactive applications—user "wait time"
- microprocessor applications—CPU time and memory requirement

3.4 information resources (e.g. database)
> documentation
> communication paths (networks)
> algorithms (as opposed to software)
> analysis techniques

training

3.6 Chances are the fit will be quite poor. The data collected by Boehm and Putnam were for large industry-grade efforts. Unless your students are in that environment, it is unlikely that a good fit will occur. Be sure to emphasize the importance of "calibrating" any empirical model before it is used.

3.8, 3.9, 3.10 A good "handout" project might be the development of software for a word processor. The following major functions could be specified:
1. user interaction
2. full screen editing
3. hardcopy document generation
3. a "dictionary" spelling checker option
5. file management system
6. peripheral control system

You might provide estimates of LOC for students and give indication of \$/LOC and LOC/person-month that would apply.

3.13 Because FP calculation is oriented toward more conventional DP applications, you might suggest a "typical" query system, data base application or payroll system as candidate projects.

3.14 This problem would make an excellent term project.

3.15 Costs and schedule are estimated early because such information is demanded (by upper management) as early as possible. If a project is extremely complex with high technological risk and a fixed price proposal is to be submitted, costing of the project should (if possible) be delayed until after requirements analysis. Note: the cost of requirements analysis alone can be estimated early.

Chapter 4
Project Management:
Planning

INTENT

The intent of this chapter is to introduce all other aspects of project management that were not covered in Chapter 3. Important topics include risk analysis, scheduling, software acquisition, re-engineering (from a management perspective) and organizational issues. The document outline for the project plan (and the Risk Management Plan) are also discussed.

Critical Points: Risk can be assessed in a systematic and statistical fashion. Distinct scheduling techniques exist and are supported by good PC-based tools. Acquisition and re-engineering are both a matter of cost justification and models for costing can be developed. A team approach for software engineering is effective.

CHAPTER OVERVIEW AND COMMENTS

Section 4.1 provides transition from Chapter 3 and introduces the need for risk analysis.

Section 4.2 introduces risk analysis. If you are teaching a management oriented course, a discussion of this topic can absorb between 1 and 2 weeks of class time. You'll need to supplement SEPA content with [BOE89] and [CHA89]. You might also cover software safety issues (see SEPA Chapter 17) at this time since safety considers the technical aspects of risks. There is a reasonably mathematical approach to this subject, see [CHA89] and this can be stressed if you have the time. Even if you cover risk lightly, it might be worthwhile to have your student do a *Risk Management and Monitoring Plan* for their course project.

Section 4.3 covers scheduling. It is important to emphasize the use of the task network as a means for laying out the project "plan of attack." Have your students develop a WBS for their project and then create the network. If at all possible, use a PC-based tool so that the dog work associated with this activity is eliminated. It also very important to emphasize the non-linear relationship between people and work. Many of my students had never heard of person-days before, and the concept of effort may be new to yours. The task network shown in Figure 4.6 was developed on MacProject II. If you'd like a copy of the task network file (you must have and Apple Macintosh and MacProject II) send me a letter along with a diskette and I'd be happy to send it to you.

Section 4.4 introduces acquisition, a subject that is becoming increasingly common in the software business. Be sure to emphasize the four options noted in Figure 4.9. The use of a decision tree is worthwhile, but be sure your students understand that the costs and probabilities are estimates only and are themselves open to substantial variation. I often find that the minute one introduces quantitative approaches in project management, the student forgets that many of the numbers are estimates and that a numerical derivation, even if it is precise, can be grossly unrealistic if the wrong values are assumed.

Section 4.5 introduces the management aspects of re-engineering. The primary focus here is on cost justification for re-engineering (for a technical discussion, see Chapter 21). This is an important issue (and will become even more important as the 1990s progress). It would be worthwhile to develop and present a numerical example that follows the steps presented in this section.

Section 4.6 introduces the team concept for software engineering. Although important, I would only recommend emphasis in management oriented courses. Otherwise, a light discussion is all that is necessary.

Section 4.7 described the *Project Plan*. All documents presented in SEPA are contained in outline form in Tables. I require my students to develop a *Project Plan* for their term project. Frankly, most students are quite disorganized (some have never worked on a team before) when it comes to conducting a long term project. By forcing them to plan, you're helping them to organize their approach. Be sure that planning is realistic!

PROBLEMS AND POINTS TO PONDER

4.1 An excellent source of information is Nancy Leveson's article on Software Safety in the *CACM*, February, 1991. Also see

[BOE89] and [CHA89].

4.2   Stated simply, most risks are, by definition, beyond the immediate control of the software project manager. The sequence of events that leads to technical risk is often difficult to foresee and eliminate; therefore, one must try to plan for the end risk, without an immediate understand of what might cause it to occur. Economic risks are a bit easier to control, but again, a contingency plan is necessary.

4.3   The risks noted here will vary depending on the status of your institutions registration system. The students will enjoy this problem because it strikes close to home.

4.7   If a project is compartmentalized and well organized; if good documentation has been done; if interfaces are clearly defined; if parallel tasks are possible; if the people who are added are generally competent; if newcomers can pick up what they need form the configuration, rather than the software engineers currently working on the project, you can add people to a project without negative impact.

4.8   The relationship can be developed by solving for t_d and varying the number of person months and duration as indicated.

4.13   Cost to make: $20.00/LOC * 5000LOC = $100,000
         Cost to buy : $50000.
         BUY !
Since 1000 LOC must be modified, cost to buy will be higher. Assume that it will cost twice as much per line to modify alien code (a conservative assumption, it could cost much, much more). Therefore:
         cost to buy = $50000 + ($40/LOC * 1000 LOC)   = $90000

still worthwhile to buy, but highly dependent on assumed cost of modification.
4.15 Use the steps presented in section 4.5, Suggest that your students develop a spreadsheet model for this analysis.

4.17   1. define specific deliverables at evenly spaced intervals (milestones)

2. reassess cost/schedule as each milestone is met
3. require intermediate reporting by senior staff
4. don't assume the 50 percent of dollars spent can be equated with 50 percent of project complete.

NOTES ON SEPA PART I

1. SEPA Chapter 1 is mandatory for all course design options.

2. See Segment 4 for a discussion of course design options and an indication of where SEPA Chapters 2 through 4 might be used.

3. Most courses offerings in CS and Computer Engineering curricula will go lightly on this part of SEPA. Actually this a bad idea. It may be that this will be the only chance your students get to understand project management issues before they move into the real world. The choice however, if often dictated by available time, which may be limited.

4. If at all possible, use CASE tools for project management to augment your lectures.

5. The *Software Engineering Teaching System* video modules entitled:
    Module 1.   Challenges of Software Development
    Module 3.   Making Software Engineering Happen
can be used to augment lectures presented for topics in this Part.

Part II

Chapter 5
Computer System
Engineering

INTENT

Computer system engineering establishes a context for software engineering. The intent of this chapter is to introduce the fundamental elements of a computer-based system and to delineate the activities that are performed by a system engineer. The basic engineering disciplines that emanate from system engineering are described and the system analysis process is presented.

Critical Points: Computer-based systems are comprised of many elements that must be systematically engineered. Computer system engineering is a process of allocation. It is out of these allocations that software requirements are derived and the software engineering process commences.

CHAPTER OVERVIEW AND COMMENTS

The fundamental elements of computer-based systems are introduced in section 5.1. It is important to emphasize that hardware and software cannot be considered in a vacuum. There are many situations where other elements are as or more important. A worthwhile topic for lecture discussion is the contrast between hardware-driven and software-driven system designs—and the problems that can result when the wrong "driver" is chosen. The hierarchical nature of systems is also a topic worth emphasizing. In fact, you might also consider discussing reuse in this context.

Section 5.2 discusses the process of allocation in the context of the CLSS example. It is important to spend time on this example because it will reappear in later chapters. Have your students come up with allocations that are not suggested in SEPA. You might even have a "Rube Goldberg" contest to see who can come up with the most novel solution to sorting.

Section 5.2.1 presents an overview of hardware engineering in the context of computer-based systems. Emphasis on this section will vary with the background and interests of your students. For in-depth coverage, supplemental readings are a must.

Section 5.2.2 presents software engineering from a chronological point of view. The flow of events depicted in Figure 5.4 will be revisited repeatedly throughout SEPA. It is worthwhile to spend time on these figures at this point. However, you should emphasize that different paradigms (see Chapter 1) might cause a different sequencing of these events, or even the elimination of one of them (e.g., the use of 4GT might eliminate the coding step). Other engineering activities are discussed in later subsections and represent a cursory introduction to human and database issues. Frankly, these topics lie outside the scope of most software engineering courses. If you have a special interest or want to emphasize one of them, you'll need supplementary material.

For a graduate level course (where outside reading is to be expected) you might assign Kidder's, *The Soul of a New Machine*. This book is, to say the least, a description of a real world antithesis to a steady engineering approach to the development of a new computer system. Nevertheless, Kidder's book is outstanding and makes an excellent discussion topic.

Section 5.3 provides a broad-brush introduction to system analysis. Each of the analysis activities and trade-off criteria noted in this section should be discussed in lecture. An interesting topic for expanded discussion is "legal considerations."

Section 5.4 presents Hatley and Pirbhai's [HAT87] architectural modeling notation. The diagrams noted can be quite useful and if time permits, you might want to work a few examples. It is important to emphasize interfaces between the regions in the AFD and the hierarchical nature of these diagrams.

An aside: Both system and software engineering requires "hierarchical thinking." This concept should be reinforced at every opportunity early in a course, because your students will need to apply it many times.

The simulation of real-time systems discussed in section 5.5 is introductory only. Further discussion is contained in Chapter 15.

The *System Specification* outline is presented in section 5.6. You might want to go over each heading with your students so that they understand what's involved in putting a spec together. The content of the System Specification (Section 2.9) will be of particular importance if you intend to begin your course project at the system stage (many users of SEPA don't do this, beginning instead with a handout System Spec). The section ends with a set of generic questions to be addressed during a system review.

Chapter 5 begins with Machiavelli's quote on the dangers associated with the introduction of a "new order". It might be worthwhile to project how computer-based systems will introduce a "new order" in the first decade of the 21st century. You might use Toeffler and/or Naisbitt as guidelines for these discussions. Topics could include: artificial intelligence, office automation, education, warfare (particularly relevant after recent experiences in the Persian Gulf), medicine, voice recognition, robots, vision systems, artificial reality, next generation personal computers, CD-ROM, networks, privacy, and general access databases.

PROBLEMS AND POINTS TO PONDER

5.1   Use a large dictionary to present the many definitions of the word. A thesaurus may help. Good luck!

5.2   You might suggest the following systems for the model requested:
    An airport
    Your university
    A bank
    A retail store

5.3   In reviewing responses to this problem, you should note highly coupled (see Chapter 10 for a software analogy) functions, completeness of I/O. For students who need suggestions, one of the following systems may be used: an airline reservation system; an operating system; a payroll system; a university registration or grade acquisition system.

5.4   System developer—knowledgeable in technology but may not be conversant in customer's domain.

Customer—understands application but may be ignorant of computing capabilities

Outsider—potentially understands both developer and customer domain but will need long learning curve.

5.5   Information (a data base); documentation; procedures

5.6   What has been done to accomplish this task previously?

Couldn't sorting occur as the boxes were packed?

Is the number of different parts (and boxes) likely to increase or decrease?

Are all boxes the same size and weight?

What is the environment in which this system will sit (e.g., corrosive, high temperature, dusty, etc.)?

Allocations: (4) Bar code reader and PC. PC prints destination on screen and a human operator does the placement into the bin; (5) Human reads box and speaks destination into vice recognition system that controls and automated shunt.

5.10 Although differences exist (e.g., a lack of a manufacturing phase for software), you should stress the similarities in discussing this problem.

5.12   The checklist should answer one global question: "Can we do it?" An example checklist follows:

    project complexity
        hardware
        software
        interfaces
   relevant staff experience
   projected degree of change
   percent "new" technology
   availability of resources
        people
        hardware
        software
  support

performance requirements

In addition to the above items, other topics considered in the book should also be added.

A "feasibility number could be calculated by assigned a numeric grade (in the range 1 to 5, say) to each attribute and a weight (same range) to be used as a multiplier for the grade. The feasibility number is the sum of the products of grade x weight.

5.13   Suggest that your students obtain one or more books on business and/or project management. The following titles should be useful:

Degarmo, E.P, et al, Engineering Economy, 7th edition, MacMillan, 1984.

DeMarco, T., Controlling Software Projects, Yourdon Press, 1982.

Gilb, T., Principles of Software Engineering Management, Addison-Wesley, 1988.

Gunther, R.C., Management Methodology for Software Product Engineering, Wiley, 1978.

Harrison, F., Advanced Project Management, Wiley, 1981.

Londiex, B., Cost Estimation for Software Development, Addison-Wesley, 1987.

Ould, M.A., Strategies for Software Engineering, Wiley, 1990.

Page-Jones, M., Practical Project Management, Dorset House Publishing, New York, 1985.

5.14   Table 2.2 rev.   Benefits for Engineering Scientific Systems
1.   More rapid acquisition of analytical data
2.   Better accuracy
3.   Ability to consider models with higher complexity, greater numbers of parameters, etc.
3.   Potential for wider choices in design synthesis
5.   More alternatives will be considered
6.   Higher interactivity between human and computer
7.   Potential for new and better data representation formats

5.18   You may, if you choose, allow students to derive their own System Specification for any of the systems shown without any handout. However, it is relatively easy to acquire a general article or paper that will serve as a consistent basis for student work. Alternatively, require that students research attributes of one of the systems, then develop the specification.

5.19 There are many cases where complete specification is impossible early in a project. In some of these, it is necessary to prototype before a formal specification can be developed. Examples are:

1. sophisticated analytical models that must be researched and developed—delay until requirements specification or even design!

2. sometimes, specific hardware/software interfaces—delay until requirements, but no later!

3. certain performance constraints—delay until requirements, but no later!

5.20   In many instances, a computer-based system is actually a "software only" system. That is, an existing standard computer, operating system and I/O environment are to be used. In such cases, the System Specification can be eliminated in lieu of a Software Requirements Specification.

There are also situations in which a system prototype (either real or paper) is much more effective than a specification.

Chapter 6
Requirements Analysis
Fundamentals

INTENT

Requirements analysis and subsequent specification of software are often the "make or break" activities in software engineering. If analysis is properly conducted, a successful design and implementation are probable. If analysis is conducted in a sloppy manner, the success of the software is doubtful.

The intent of this chapter is to lay a conceptual foundation for the analysis techniques described in Chapters 7 through 9. Basic analysis responsibilities and concepts are described, fundamental analysis principles are presented, and the structure and format of the requirements specification are discussed.

Critical Points: Software analysis, regardless of the method and notation that is used, applies four fundamental principles: analysis of the information domain, functional, behavioral and information modeling, partitioning, and logical/physical modeling. Successful analysis demands application of all four.

CHAPTER OVERVIEW AND COMMENTS

Section 6.1 discusses the tasks and responsibilities associated with requirements analysis. Be sure to emphasize Figure 6.1 during lecture. That is, it is important to emphasize that some software analysis activities are performed during system engineering; others are performed during design. Conversely, a bit of system engineering and more than a little design are often performed during software requirements analysis. As much as your student would like to make it happen, there is no distinct boundary between these activities; rather, there is a hazy transition from one to the next. The categorization of the activity (Is it analysis or design?) is not nearly so important as the fact that the activity is conducted.

Section 6.2 emphasizes the importance of communication during analysis and the problems that result when communication breaks down. You should stress the veracity of the "First Law of System Engineering." Students should recognize that change is a way of life in the software business.

Section 6.3 stressed methods for improving customer communication. I would strongly recommend that you try FAST techniques for the *SafeHome* system (SEPA, p. 183) or you can use FAST techniques effectively as you define requirements for term projects. Let some of your student play the role of marketing types and other play the role of engineers. Follow the guidelines defined for FAST.

Section 6.4 presents the fundamental analysis principles. This discussion is crucial and should be reinforced during lecture. It seems that essential/implementation (logical / physical) modeling often causes confusion for students. You might assign readings from [MCM84] for another point of view.

Today, many professionals recognize that written specification is often a difficult (and sometimes undesirable) way to represent the results of analysis. Section 6.5 presents an alternative—prototyping. I often have the students develop a simple paper prototype for a human interface (e.g., a video game, a desk-top publishing system, an expert system). For graduate courses, Section 6.5.2 should be supplemented with outside readings and given considerably more emphasis. Each of the topics noted in this section are worthy of at least one lecture hour (at the graduate level).

Section 6.6 presents a rather detailed discussion of *Software Requirements Specification*. The principles noted in Section 6.6.1, although originally focused on formal specification languages, apply quite well to less formal written specs. Your students will undoubtedly have questions on the content of the *Software Requirements Specification* described in Section 6.6.3, with particular focus on what you expect from them for their term project. You should be very specific in your desired. You must hold their hand on this or chaos will result! You should describe your requirements for each section during lecture. I put two or three (of the best) document sets from past years' projects on reserve at the library. Students are encouraged to review them to get a feeling for content and style.

Although Section 6.7 is brief, it should not be glossed over. It is important for your students to understand the importance of review at each step in the software engineering process. In fact, you might want to have them read Chapter 17 at this time, so that each project team can conduct proper formal technical reviews.

PROBLEMS AND POINTS TO PONDER

6.1   Refer to the last sentence in the introduction to this chapter.
- Customer doesn't completely understand what is desired
- final result is hazy
- analyst cannot understand customer's world
- personality conflict between analyst and customer
- too many customers

6.2   One or more constituencies who will be using the new software feel "threatened" by it in some way, e.g., it may threaten jobs; provide greater management control; attack "tradition." One way to reduce (but rarely eliminate) problems is to introduce the rationale for a new system early, and educate users so that the threat of the unknown is reduced.

6.3   Although "ideal" analysts are a rare breed, the following attributes would be nice:
    - conversant in both customer and developer world
    - excellent communication skills
    - good technical computing background

6.4   The customer for information systems is often another department in the same company—often referred to as the "user department." The customer for computer based products is typically the marketing department! The customer for computer-based systems may be an internal department, marketing or an outside entity (e.g., a government agency, another company, an end-user).

6.7   The *Preliminary User Manual* is a form of paper prototype for the software that is to be built. It provides the reader with a characterization of the software taken from the user's point of view.

6.8   Because the customer doesn't know everything on day 1. Also, as the requirements begin to crystallize, the customer gains greater insight, thereby seeing things that were previously "invisible."

6.9 The information domain for *SafeHome* should be organized hierarchically:
- user input information
- entry code
- bounding levels
- phone numbers
- delay times
- sensor information
- break-in

... etc.

You might introduce a DFD (see Chapter 7) like notation for representing flow, or delay consideration of this until later.

6.10 Partitioning will depend on the requirements established by the students. Be sure that each level of the function hierarchy represents the same level of detail. For example, a function such as read sensor input should not be at the same level (in the hierarchy) as dial telephone number. The latter is a reasonably low level function, while the former encompasses many important activities. Teach your students to think hierarchically!

6.11 - 6.14   The remainder of these problems might best be left for a term project.

6.15 It is extremely useful to compare the requirements derived by different students. The lesson learned is that even when the problem statement is identical, there is much room for interpretation. Hence, a critical need for review with your customer.

Chapter **7**
Structured Analysis
and Its Extensions

INTENT

In the preceding chapter, the fundamental concepts of requirements analysis and specification were presented. In this chapter, our focus shifts to the most widely used requirements analysis method—structured analysis (SA). The majority of software engineering courses teach structured analysis as the method of choice, using SA notation and heuristics as a base from which other methods (presented in Chapters 8 and 9) can be taught.

There was a time when SA was used strictly by the IS community and was shunned by developers of engineering and technical software. However, the development of extensions to SA, presented in this chapter, make the method amenable to the modeling needs demanded by real-time systems.

Critical Points: The structured analysis method is a modeling technique that shares the set of fundamental analysis principles that were described in Chapter 6. The method introduces a notation for modeling the information domain, representing behavior, function and information, partitioning the problem that software is to solve, and representing both essential and implementation models. The flow models created as part of SA can be mapped directly (see Chapter 11) into an architectural design for the software.

CHAPTER OVERVIEW AND COMMENTS

Section 7.1 presents a brief history of the evolution of SA, indicating how the method has broadened its focus over the past two decades. You might want to complement this discussion with a presentation on the evolution of CASE tools that address SA.

Section 7.2 and 7.3 introduce the SA method. First, the

notation is presented (in section 7.2)—the data flow diagram (DFD), extensions for modeling real-time systems, the CSPEC, PSPEC, STD, and other forms. In section 7.3, the mechanics of SA are presented in the context of the *SafeHome* problem. I have found the the "grammatical parse (SEPA, p. 222) is well received by students, who use it to get started in their diagramming. You should stress the approach. (by the way, it's also a first cut at object-oriented thinking, something that will be stressed in the next chapter. Generally, these sections absorb at least two to three hours of lecture, with appropriate examples. Points to emphasize:

• Students are often confused about the difference between data and control flow. You should use additional examples to make the difference obvious.
• The CSPEC and STDs may be new to your student and their understanding of the behavioral view (as opposed to a functional view) may be confused. Be sure to spend time here.
• Do not leave these sections until you are convinced that students are conversant with the notation and method. It is a good idea to assign a homework problem that forces development of a flow models and other model components—it looks simpler than it is!

Section 7.4 discusses the requirements dictionary (the terms requirements dictionary and data dictionary are used interchangeably throughout SEPA). You might want to foreshadow the project database (Chapter 21) and/or the repository (Chapter 23) at this point. It is critically important to stress the benefits that can be derived by where-used/how used information.

Section 7.5 should be supplemented with classroom demonstrations of the SA tools that you have acquired as part of the Software Engineering Teaching System (Segment 2 of the *Instructor's Manual*). In addition, reference to Chapter 22 might be useful at this time.

PROBLEMS AND POINTS TO PONDER

7.2 Flow diagrams and the requirements dictionary enable the software engineer to represent flow and content of the information domain. The CSPEC and STD enable behavioral elements of a system to be represented. Flow models, CSPECS, PSPECS and the dictionary encourage partitioning. Representation of data stores, and external entities is one way to represent aspects of the implementation model.

7.3 Information flow indicates how data and control are transformed as they move through a system (from input to output) Information structure indicates the organization of data and control.

7.4 Be sure that models produced indicate major input and output information and any databases that is required (Note: many people believe that the context level DFD should not represent data stores; I don't feel that this restriction is necessary.) At the undergraduate level, you might suggest systems like: course registration; dormitory assignments; the library; the work study or co-op system; financial aid, etc.

7.5 If students have background in compilers or operating systems, suggest one of these as a DFD exercise. Otherwise, propose any one of the following:
- an income tax package
- a suite of statistics functions
- a popular video game
- a flight controller for an aircraft
- any system relevant to your students

Be sure to emphasize the importance of a hierarchical approach to function partitioning when functions are defined.

7.7 Not necessarily. For example, a composite data item can be shown as input to a level 0 transform. The composite item is refined in the requirements dictionary into three elementary data items that are each shown separately at a refinement indicated at level 1. Even though the names of the flow items have changes and their number has changed, flow continuity is maintained through the dictionary.

7.8. Ward and Mellor use a "control transform" in the place of the CSPEC and provide detailed of the control transform in the processing narrative that accompanies the transform. The use of the STD is the same, although it is not "attached" to a CSPEC.

7.9 A control process is accommodated with Hatley-Pirbhai using the CSPEC and (possibly) a PAT.

7.10 Event flow indicates that something has occurred. In most cases the occurrence can be represented either by a true/false condition or by a limited number of discrete values.

7.12 You might suggest that your students approach the problem using the grammatical parse (object-oriented thinking) described in this chapter. You can also use this problem to illustrate data modeling techniques presented in Chapter 8.

The following data objects should be identified for PHTRS and reorganized into 1NF, 2NF, 3NF (see SEPA Chapter 8)

    pot hole data
        identifying number
        street address
        size
        location in street
        district *
        repair priority *
    work order data:
        pot hole location
        size
        repair crew ID number
        number of people in crew
        equipment assigned
        hours applied
        hole status
        amount of filler used
        cost of repair *
    damage data
        citizen's name
        citizen's address
        citizens phone number
        type of damage
        dollar claim

Note that those objects followed by a * can be derived from other objects. Be sure that students properly define the various normal forms.

This problem is amenable to data flow, data structured (chapter 9) and object-oriented (Chapter 8) analysis approaches. If time permits (it usually doesn't unless you're conducting a two term course) it is worthwhile to have students solve the problem using both analysis methods.

Chapter 8
Object-Oriented Analysis and Data Modeling

INTENT

Object-oriented (O^2) thinking is the current "hot topic" within the software engineering community. To date, the majority of work conducted at both universities and in industry has been object-oriented programming—a journey back to the old days when people just "wrote code." Over the last few years there has been a an attempt to codify an approach to object-oriented analysis (this chapter) and object-oriented design (Chapter 12).

The intent of this chapter is to introduce the concepts that underlie object-oriented thinking and the basic approach used to accomplish data modeling. The two topics, although different in many ways, are connected by a concentration on objects, as opposed to disjointed data and process—the view of the old school.

I have chosen the Coad and Yourdon notation for OOA, not because I think that it will necessarily become the predominant notation for O^2 modeling (it's too early to tell which notation will predominate), but because it is representative of many similar modeling approaches, is relative easy to learn, and illustrates the basic concepts that are relevant to OOA. The use of E-R diagramming techniques are well established in the IS community, but are only beginning to penetrate the engineering and technical space.

Critical Points: OOA focuses on the definition of classes and their attributes. Operations that are relevant to a class are also defined. Object are instantiated from classes and inherit their attributes and operations. Guidelines exist for identifying classes/objects and a notation—called OOA—can be used to represent relationships among classes/objects. Data modeling focuses solely on data (to the exclusion of operations) but used the same object-oriented point of view. The E-R diagram defines data objects and their relationships to one another.

CHAPTER OVERVIEW AND COMMENTS

Section 8.1 introduces basic object-oriented concepts and is essential for any course in software engineering (whether or not you intend to stress this topic and even if the course is management focused). At least one lecture hour should be spent on this section, even if the remainder of the chapter is to be given light brush treatment. This section is a prerequisite for Chapter 12. You might assign homework that forces your students to practice defining objects for real-world software problems. This looks easier than it is. It remains worthwhile to use the "grammatical parse" on a processing narrative as a way to accomplish this.

Be certain that all key O^2 terms are introduced and understood by your students. They should feel comfortable defining class, object, attribute, operations, message, etc. They should also be aware of the criteria through which object selections are made. I would suggest giving a pop quiz during the class session immediately after this lecture. Ask for all definitions to drive their importance home.

Section 8.2 introduces the Coad and Yourdon notation for OOA. The diagrammatic notation itself is not as important as the concepts it introduces. Be sure your students recognize the hierarchy of classification implied by a classification (assembly) structure. The use of a *subject* is sometimes confusing to students; be sure they understand that it's nothing more than the O^2 equivalent of a PSPEC that contains other diagrammatic notation, rather than procedural detail.

Cardinality notation is introduced in section 8.2.3 and will be of use later in this chapter. If you intend to cover data modeling (section 8.3), you should spend some time here.

Section 8.3 present data modeling as a technique and E-R diagramming as a notation. Space constraints have caused me to give this superficial treatment (entire books have been written on the subject) and for that reason, supplementary reading (see **Further Readings** for suggestions) is recommended if you intend to stress the content of this section. If time permits (e.g., a two term course), it might be worthwhile to introduce object-oriented databases at this point. Gupta and Horowitz (eds.) (*Object-Oriented Databases with Applications for CASE, Networks and VLSI CAD,* Prentice-Hall, 1991) present excellent coverage of this subject.

PROBLEMS AND POINTS TO PONDER

8.2, 8.3 A good source of information on the "real" answer to this question can be found in Meyer's book (see **Further Readings**).

8.4 A <u>class</u> is a categorization of any of the objects listed on SEPA p. 242. <u>Inheritance</u> is like a template for attributes and operations. The template is overlaid on an object definition, enabling the object to use all attributes and operations defined for its class. <u>Encapsulation</u> is a packaging mechanism—it allows the analysis to combine data and process and refer to them with the same name.

8.6 See discussion of problem 7.12. Objects and attributes are implied by the list shown.

8.7 – 8.10 Any of these problems would make worthwhile term projects, but be careful here. If students choose this approach, they will have to supplement the SEPA O^2 presentation with readings from additional references. See **Further Readings** for Chapters 8 and 12 for suggestions.

FAST can be viewed as a O^2 approach in that the lists suggested for FAST can take on an O^2 flavor.

8.11 Messaging is language dependent. This problem, if you choose to use it, might be delayed until the O^2 design presentation in Chapter 12.

8.12 If time permits, you might use this problem (in a graduate course) as a catalyst for a discussion of the components classification issue. This is one of the most important areas of research in the O^2 domain. It remains a major roadblock to achieving effective reuse when the O^2 paradigm is used.

8.13 The primary difference between an OOA object and a data modeling object is encapsulation. A data object, packages data only. A true object (in the O^2 sense) packages both data and process (operations).

Chapter 9
Alternative Analysis Techniques and Formal Methods

INTENT

The intent of this chapter is twofold: (1) to provide an introduction to analysis methods that use a data structure-oriented view, rather than a data flow point of few, and (2) to introduce the student to formal specification methods. It could be argued that this chapter presented "old thinking" and "new thinking."

To be frank, data structured-oriented analysis methods are beginning to fall by the wayside and could arguably be called old thinking in the analysis modeling area. I have de-emphasized the presentation of this topic in this edition of SEPA. Most professors who used SEPA 2/e did not cover this material, but continued to recommend its inclusion in the text for completeness.

Formal specification methods, on the other hand, represent what many believe is "new thinking" in analysis modeling. I have attempted to provide the student with the flavor other formal specification and have included a reprint of a paper by Michael Spivey that is one of the better examples of the application of this important new technology. Many universities have begun to emphasize formalism. If your department has taken a "formal" approach, you'll need to supplement this Chapter with additional readings.

CHAPTER OVERVIEW AND COMMENTS

Section 9.1 reviews the characteristics that are common among all analysis methods and then discussed those things that differentiate these methods. This is an important topic and it would be worthwhile assigning this section, even if you intend to skip the remained of the discussion of data structure oriented methods.

Section 5.3 introduces data structure oriented methods for requirements analysis. The relationship between data structure oriented techniques and object-oriented approaches should not be overlooked.

Data Structured Systems Development (DSSD) is presented in Section 9.3. In reality, Ken Orr presented DSSD in three voluminous manuals. All we can hope to accomplish in this section is to make the student aware of the basic approach and terminology and more importantly, to make the student aware that more than one point of view exists. Be sure that the student recognizes the difference between the entity diagram and the data flow diagram.

Like DSSD, the Jackson System Development method (Section 9.4) really demands a dedicated textbook for complete explication. My purpose in the section is identical to the one expressed for section 9.3. Although Jackson has a penchant for introducing arcane and sometimes confusing terminology and notation, his approach is really quite powerful. A lecture dedicated to JSD might be justified at the graduate level. Use [JAC83] or [CAM89] (from SEPA Chapter 13) as a source of supplementary information.

Section 9.5 presents an overview of SADT. If you choose to stress this method, I would recommend readings from [MAR88].

Formal specification is another hot topic in the software engineering community today. Sections 9.6 introduces the basic concepts that underlie formal specification. If you want to introduce your students to some of the mathematics that underlie these approaches (be careful, this can be time consuming and is probably better left to a course that is dedicated to these methods), I would recommend using one or more of the books on formal methods listed in Appendix I. The discussion of abbreviated discussion of formal language attributes lays the foundation for the next section.

Section 9.6 presents a detailed example of the Z specification language as it has been applied to the specification of an operating system kernel. Depending on the background of your students, it might be worthwhile to provide a brief tutorial on OS internals before proceeding with this section. I suspect that some professors may decide to walk through section 9.6 in lecture. If time permits, I recommend this approach. Space constraints in this edition of SEPA have caused me to spend relatively little space on proof of correctness as it relates to formal specification. If you are so inclined, this would be an ideal time to introduce this topic.

Section 9.8 presents an abbreviated overview of a number of automated approaches to requirements analysis and specification. Any one of the methods/tools discussed could be used in expanded lecture presentation, but time will likely preclude this approach.

PROBLEMS AND POINTS TO PONDER

9.1 Because the DSSD is based on a hierarchical view of information structure, partitioning of information and function is inherent in is achieved in Warnier-Orr diagrams and assembly diagrams. Entity diagrams provide a flow-oriented view, but it is important to recognize the difference between them and DFDs. [There are no transforms represented in the entity diagram.] Behavioral representation is not explicitly shown and control oriented representation can be implied, but is not explicit.

9.2 It could be argued that JSD is really closer to OOA that it is to flow-oriented techniques. It implements the basic principles in a roundabout fashion, but all fundamentals do exist. The entity structure steps partitions and models information (and by implication, function) in a hierarchical fashion. The initial model step takes a data and control flow view—the use of data stream and state vector connections accomplish this. Behavioral modeling is not explicitly noted diagrammatically, but is implied with structure text. In reality the JSD analysis steps are continued right to code therefore essence leads to implementation in a direct way.

9.4 through 9.9 It is unlikely that you will have time to assign these problems, if you also require a term project. If they are assigned, be certain to have references on reserve at your library so that students can gain additional insight into these analysis methods.

9.10 and 9.11 It is unlikely that you will have time to assign these problems, if you also require a term project. If they are assigned, you will have to spend substantially more lecture time on formal methods and will have to be certain to have references on reserve at your library so that students can gain additional insight into formal methods.

Part III

Chapter 10
Software Design Fundamentals

INTENT

Design lies at the technical kernel of software engineering. For this reason, most instructors allocate the majority of all lecture time to design issues. The intent of this chapter is to provide the student with some of the answers to the questions: "What is a "good" computer program? How do I judge its quality? What can I do to develop high quality programs myself?

It is likely that the student has encountered some of the topics presented in this chapter in earlier Computer Science courses. However, the topics are so important that a bit of redundancy is worthwhile. Other topics will be encountered for the first time and should be emphasized.

This chapter also presents an overview of structured programming and procedural design, introducing PDL and other design representation forms. It is important that the student understand that procedural design always occurs after data and architectural design (described in subsequent chapters). I've broken with chronological sequence and presented the topic here for purposes of clarity.

Critical Points: A set of fundamental characteristics enables us to assess the quality of a design regardless of the software application area or programming language that is used. Software design is a multistep, multi-method process that results in a reviewable design representation. The structured programming philosophy is central to procedural design. A number of different notational schemes may be used to represent logical detail.

CHAPTER OVERVIEW AND COMMENTS

Section 10.1 introduces the development phase of the software engineering process and foreshadows more thorough treatments of each step in the chapters that follow. Note the emphasis on quality and the impact that design has on quality.

Section 10.2 discusses both the technical and management aspects of design. A brief history is presented in section 10.2.2. For a graduate course, it may be worthwhile to assign some of the "historical references" as supplementary readings.

Section 10.3 (one of the more important sections in all of SEPA!) presents a reasonably detailed discussion of fundamental concepts that affect good design. Depending on the background of your students, much of this material may have already been encountered in earlier courses. It should still be reviewed! If you feel that your students are weak in any of these areas, extra emphasis should be given during lecture and/or further outside readings should be assigned.

Section 10.4 discusses effective module design and introduces the concepts of cohesion and coupling. Although these two module attributes are categorized at a number of different levels, it is not critically important to have the student be capable of identifying a specific level. Rather, the student should understand that a spectrum exists and that he/she should strive for low coupling and high cohesion.

Data design (Section 10.5) lies at the heart of effective software design. Unfortunately, a comprehensive discussion of data design would require a detailed presentation of data structures and is beyond the scope of SEPA. You may want to augment the material in this section with other material from a Data Structures course. If your students have a firm foundation in data structures (and related topics) the presentation here should be sufficient.

Architectural design (Section 10.6) is a topic that is often glossed over in other computer Science Courses. This is unfortunate because the software architecture has much to do with the implementability, testability and maintainability of a program. The design methods introduced in the following chapters focus on the derivation of software architecture.

Procedural design (Section 10.7) is closely related to "programming" and should be well understood by your students. Most will have already be indoctrinated into structured programming practice and will be familiar with one or more procedural design tools. The PDL introduced in section 10.7.4 can be extended and/or modified to meet your purposes (e.g., you might want to create a PDL based on the programming language that most of your students use (iff it's a modern, high-order language!).

The *Design Specification* (Section 10.8) is the most important document generated during the development phase. You should present each section in detail, giving examples from various application areas.

PROBLEMS AND POINTS TO PONDER

10.1 Yes, but the design is conducted implicitly—often in a haphazard manner. During design we develop representations of programs—not the programs themselves.

10.2 We create a functional hierarchy and as a result refine the problem. For example, considering the check writer, we might write:

```
Refinement 1:
    write dollar amount in words

Refinement 2:
    procedure write_amount;
        validate amount is within bounds;
        parse to determine each dollar unit;
        generate alpha representation;
    end write_amount

Refinement 3:
    procedure write_amount;
        do while checks remain to be printed
            if dollar amount > upper amount bound
                then print "amount too large error message;
                else set process flag true;
            endif;
            determine maximum significant digit;
            do while (process flag true and significant
                digits remain)
                set for corresponded alpha phrase;
                divide to determine whole number value;
                concatenate partial alpha string;
                reduce significant digit count by one;
            enddo
```

```
            print alpha string;
         enddo
      end write_amount
```

10.3   There are cases in which different parts of a problem are interrelated in a manner that makes separate considerations more complex than combined considerations. Highly coupled problems exhibit this characteristic. However, continuing combination of problem parts cannot go on indefinitely because the amount of information exceeds one's ability to understand. Therefore, when (10.2) is not true, modularity may be modified, but not eliminated.

10.4   In some time critical applications, monolithic implementation may be required. However, design can and should occur as if the software was to be implemented modularly. Then "modules" are coded in-line.

10.5   See section 10.3.7.

10.6   The robot controller:

Abstraction I:
   The software will incorporate control functions that will allow manipulation of a robot arm using instructions obtained form disk storage. The instructions will control x, y, z motion, pitch and roll motion, gripper (the robot hand) action and force sensing by the arm.

Abstraction II:
   Robot Software Tasks:
      Instruction input interface;
      Instruction processor;
      Command output interface;
      Feedback controller;
end.

Abstraction III:
   sub-task: instruction processor
      obtain an instruction;
      determine instruction type;
         assess potential conflicts;

```
            process instruction;
        end.
```

Abstraction IV:
```
    procedure: process instruction;
        case of <instruction-type>;
            when <instruction-type is motion> select
                motion-calculations;
            when <instruction-type is gripper> select
                gripper-control;
            when <instruction-type is sensing> select
                read sensing ports;
        end case
        test error-flags prior to instruction execution;
        execute instruction;
    end
```

Abstraction V:
```
    procedure: motion calculations;
        case of <motion-type>;
            when <motion-type is linear> select
            begin: compute linear motion from (x,y,z)
                start to (x,y,z);
                apply accel/decel information to path ;
                test violations of arm travel bounds;
                set  flags as required;
            end
        when ... end
```

10.7   Parnas' seminal paper has been reproduced in a number of anthologies of important software engineering papers (e.g., Yourdon's *Classics in Software Engineering* or the IEEE tutorial by Freeman and Wasserman, *Software Design Techniques*. Parnas uses a KWIC index system as an example. To quote from his description:

The KWIC index system accepts an ordered set of lines, each line is an ordered set of words and each word is an ordered set of characters. A line may be "circularly shifted" by repeatedly removing the first word and appending it to the end of the line. The KWIC index system outputs a listing of all circular shifts of all lines in alphabetical order.

Note: In the late 1980s, Parnas was embroiled in the debate over the viability of software for DoD's Strategic Defense Initiative (SDI). If this issue is still current at the time that you are using SEPA, his arguments concerning software quality and reliability and software safety in the context of SDI would make excellent classroom discussion.

10.8   Information hiding can be related to both coupling and cohesion concepts. By limiting the availability of information to only those modules that have absolute need, coupling between modules is inherently reduced. In general, isolation of information predicates isolation of function; therefore, cohesion of individual modules can also be improved.

10.10 Common coupling is increased when a programming language supports internal procedures and as a consequence, information hiding is difficult to achieve (although the spirit of the concept can be maintained).

10.11   External world, compiler, and operating system coupling will affect software portability adversely. As an example, consider a program that has been designed to make use of special graphics features of an intelligent terminal. If the software is moved to a system without the terminal, major design and code modifications may be required.

10.13 - 10.21   Many of these problems are programming classics. Solutions can be found in any of a number of programming text books. In general, I emphasize the use of PDL and recommend that students use it for their design representations. If you do this, be sure that the design is not really "source code in disguise." That is, the design should be reasonably detailed but should be represented at a level of abstraction that is one step above code.

Chapter 11
Data Flow-Oriented Design

INTENT

This chapter presents a data flow-oriented design method—often referred to as *structured design*—that may be used to develop program structure from a set of DFDs (Chapter 7) generated from requirements analysis. The technique is relatively simple, building upon concepts introduced in Chapter 7.

The structured design technique is the most widely used approach for the derivation of architectural design. It is extremely simple to learn and apply and is recommended for course projects. However, you should note that design methods introduced in Chapters 12, 13, 14 and 15 each have their place, and may be an appropriate alternative to structured design.

Critical Points: It is possible to map data flow into a program structure (architecture) in a systematic manner. This enables us to trace requirements analysis representations directly into design.

CHAPTER OVERVIEW AND COMMENTS

Section 11.1 describes the evolution of data flow oriented design and indicates major areas of application. It is important to note that data flow techniques may be applied in all software application areas. For graduate level courses, selected readings from references [MYE78] or [YOU78] (at the time of this writing, Ed Yourdon is completing a newly revised edition of his book on structured design; it will likely be published by Prentice-Hall with a 1993 copyright) may be used to supplement material in this chapter.

The design process is driven by characteristics of data flow for a specific problem. In section 11.2 transform and transaction flow are described and an overview of the data flow design approach is presented. You should note that all flows may be viewed as transform, but obvious transaction flow should be mapped using transaction analysis.

Sections 11.3 and 11.4 present a step-by-step approach to

transform analysis and transaction analysis. The *SafeHome* example should be discussed in detail during lecture. The use of both transform and transaction structures within a given application is also discussed. This concept is sometimes confusing to students. You should supplement SEPA with additional examples during lecture. Note that unnecessary control modules almost always develop and must be eliminated when combined structures are defined.

A set of design heuristics that can prove useful when refining the program structure is presented in Section 11.5. When discussing these guidelines, it may be worthwhile to refer back to the fundamental design concepts presented in Chapter 10.

Section 11.6 describes design activities that must occur after the program structure has been derived. You should emphasize that both structure derivation and related design documentation are an essential part of the design process.

Design optimization (Section 11.7) is treated only briefly in SEPA. Additional material on optimization may be obtained from many of the references to this chapter.

PROBLEMS AND POINTS TO PONDER

11.2 When transform mapping is used where transaction map-ping should be used, two problems arise: (1) the program structure tends to become top heavy with control modules—these should be eliminated; (2) significant data coupling occurs because information associated with one of many "processing actions" must be passed to an outgoing path.

11.4 Proposed approaches to the problem of real time design must take into account the non-sequential processing that occurs as a consequence of interrupts and the possibility that a non-hierarchical structure might better satisfy an application. These and other characteristics of real-time software design are discussed in detail in Chapter 15.

11.5 Classic examples include:
   -   many engineering analysis algorithms
   -   many process control applications
   -   some commercial applications
Look for a well-developed DFD and correct mapping to program

structure.

11.6   Classic examples include:
-       compilers
-       most interactive systems (e.g. CAD systems)
-       all menu-driven applications
Look for well-developed DFD and correct mapping to program structure.

11.8   The following books provide necessary details on compiler design:
Aho, A.V., R. Sethi and J.D. Ullman, Compilers: Principles, Techniques and Tools, Addison-Wesley, 1985.
Fischer, C.N. and R.J. Le Blanc, Crafting a Compiler, Addison-Wesley, 1990.
Holub, A.I, Compiler Design in C, Prentice-Hall, 1990.
Tremblay, J.P. and Sorenson, The Theory and Practice of Compiler Writing, McGraw-Hill, 1985.

11.9   The data flow representation for recursive applications will loop back on itself. However, there is no reason why a recursive module or modules cannot be integrated into the structures described in this chapter.

11.10   The structure mapped from the DFD for this problem is shown in the figure on the following page. It is important to emphasize that extraneous control modules should be removed from the mapping.

11.11 For each of the categories noted in the problem statement:
a)   problems can occur if interrupts are processed, but generally applicable; extensions do exist
b)   good technique as are others
c)   applicable but data structure or object oriented technique should also be considered
d)   indeterminacy of I/O and heavy emphasis on table-driven functions could present problems, better to use object-oriented
e)   good technique as is data structure oriented
f)   OK to use, but object-oriented design probably better
g)   excellent technique
h)   good technique (transaction oriented)
 i)   some comments as (a)
j)   same comments as (f)

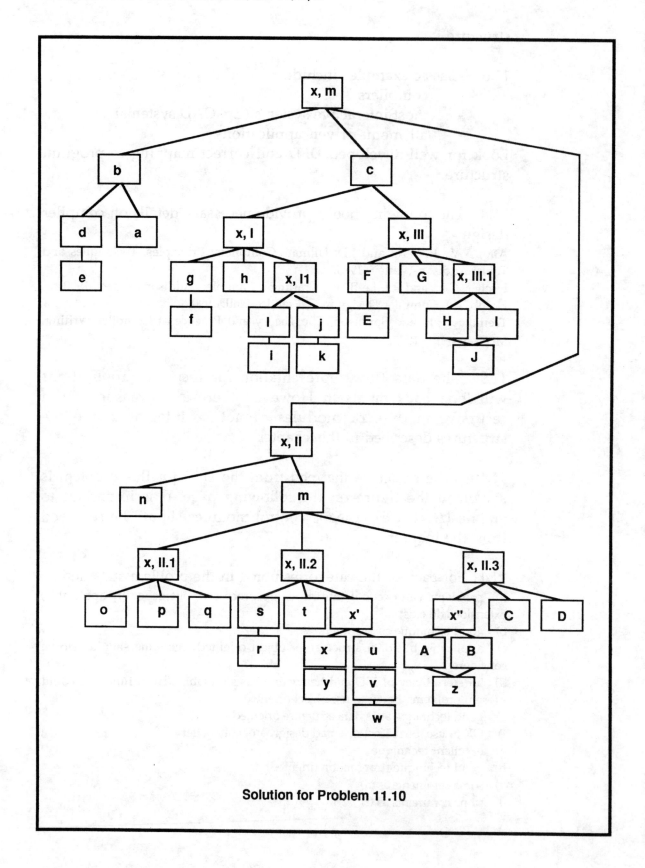

Solution for Problem 11.10

11.13 Data structure

11.14 The following attributes require "optimization:"
1. execution speed
2. memory requirement
3. numerical accuracy

Brief Discussion: A modular approach enables those modules that are "processor-bound" to be refined for greater efficiency (e.g. a better algorithm, recode in a more efficient language). By defining the structure first, common processing can be exploded and memory requirements reduced. Similarly, an understanding of the software structure can result in more controlled transfer of data and less likelihood of unintentional numerical errors.

Chapter 12
Object-Oriented Design

INTENT

Although the underlying concepts of object-oriented programming have been with us for almost two decades, it is only over the past five years that the approach has generated intense interest in the software engineering community. Today, OOD is *tres chic*. Unlike some fads, however, I believe OOD has significant merit and may become the software development approach of preference during the 1990s.

The intent of this chapter is to introduce the student to the basic philosophy, terminology and concepts of object-oriented design. After reading this chapter (as well as Chapter 8) and attending lecture, the student should appreciate (1) that OOD is a different and powerful approach to design; (2) the concepts of classes, objects, messages, operations, inheritance, encapsulation, etc., and (3) a notation for representing object-oriented design models.

Some users of SEPA will undoubtedly focus on object-oriented techniques (to the general exclusion of Chapters 11 and 13). If you want to emphasize OOD to the exclusion of other methods (while at the same time using SEPA) you'll need: (1) a good supplementary text (e.g., [BOO90] or [MEY90]) and (2) access to an object oriented programming language (e.g., Smalltalk).

Critical Points: Software may be represented as a set of classes and objects that are manipulated by operations. To invoke an operation, an object is sent a message. OOD introduces notation for defining class and object relationships, modularizing the design and allocating objects to different processors. The heuristics for object-oriented design include an identification of data abstractions and the operations that must act on them.

CHAPTER OUTLINE AND COMMENTS

Object-oriented design has evolved from a number of disparate sources. In fact, even today, there are different views of what

OOD is, what an O^2 language is, and how the approach should be best applied. In section 12.1, the origins of OOD are described. It is important to note that the "classic" view of OOD has evolved from the Smalltalk approach. Over the past ten years, the emphasis on Ada has precipitated another more limited view of OOD.

Section 12.2 reviews the key terminology and concepts of OOD (many of these were first introduced in Chapter 8). Although these ideas are not intellectually difficult, it is possible that your students may find them a bit confusing (unless they have had prior experience with O^2 languages). For this reason, lecture time should be dedicated to the ideas contained in this section.

Sections 12.3 through 12.6 present an OOD approach that was popularized by Booch [BOO83] and then extended to accommodate analysis (OOA) by Coad and Yourdon. The categorization and refinement implied by this discussion is crucial to effective OOD.

The "noun-verb" approach has already been introduced in SEPA. Here, I describe the approach in a more rigorous fashion. It turns out that this approach can be useful during both analysis and design and can be used in conjunction with other design methods (e.g., data flow, Jackson, DSSD). For this reason, your students should be encouraged to apply it.

Section 12.7 introduces Booch's notation for OOD. This section provides an overview only. If you intend to present this in lecture, you'll need a copy of [BOO90] to get the additional information necessary for further discussion. The key point to make (even if you spend little time here) are that (1) classes can be related to one another in a variety of ways; (2) objects communicate in different ways and a notation can be developed to represent this; (3) the Booch diagram encapsulates the object definition, and (4) in multiprocessor systems, it is possible to assign objects to different processors.

Section 12.8 illustrates the fact that detail O^2 design is similar to all types of procedural design—procedural information is represented using a notation (e.g., PDL) the enables algorithms to be specified.

Section 12.9 presents a an alternate approach and more classical approach to OOD. Here, the fundamental O^2 concepts of inheritance, messages, objects and operations are derived using a procedure that is predicated on the specification of data abstractions..

In many instances (no pun intended!), both OOD approaches can be applied (at the risk of some confusion). The Booch approach is best applied during analysis and early design. The more classical OOD approach may be effectively applied during analysis and intermediate levels of design.

There are many people who desperately want to meld SA/SD and O^2 techniques. Personally, I have reservations about this, but section 12.10 presents a quick overview of current thinking.

PROBLEMS AND POINTS TO PONDER

12.1   We live in a world of objects and classes. Hundreds of examples are possible:

class: furniture
    objects:
        chair
        sofa
        desk
        table
        ottoman
class: buildings
    objects:
        apartment building
        office building
        warehouse
        residential dwelling
        factory
... and so on.

12.2 Conventional programming languages such as FORTRAN lack all of the key elements that make a programming language object-oriented. They do not have the ability to define data abstractions—a key for the definition of classes and objects; they have no means to achieve inheritance; they have no dynamic binding capability, making messages difficult to implement.

12.5 The underlying concepts of OOD demand some connection with a specific programming language. How are objects defined? How is inheritance implemented? How are messages passed and defined? A knowledge of the implementation language is necessary to answer these questions.

12.5 through 12.11   If you intend to have your students attempt one or more of these problems, I would recommend assigning specific problems with a specific O^2 approach. For example, you might try problem 12.6 using the Booch approach and problem 12.8 using the alternative approach presented in Section 12.9.

Chapter 13
Data -Oriented Design Methods

INTENT

This chapter introduces a third "school" of software design—mapping techniques that transform information structure into a design representation of software. An overview of the Jackson methodology and DSSD is presented. Although each of these techniques is more complex than the data flow-oriented approach, many contend that the resultant design is more robust.

DSSD can be categorized as data structure-oriented with no real confusion. However, the Jackson methodology is difficult to place in any category (some would call it object-oriented). I have placed JSD in this chapter because the underlying program design approach (JSP) makes heavy use of data structures to derive the procedural hierarchy of programs.

The intent of this chapter is to provide the student with a working knowledge of each of these important design methods. However, supplementary readings and substantial lecture time must be expended if the student is to be able to apply one or more of these techniques to real-word problems. The vast majority of professors who have adopted SEPA do not cover this material in class.

Critical Points: Data (information) structure can have a profound impact on the design of software. The structure of information must be considered as part of software design. A number of different methods, each with different terminology and notation, but all with the same underlying philosophy, are available to transform data structure into program design.

CHAPTER OVERVIEW AND COMMENTS

Sections 13.1 and 13.2 introduce the concept of data-oriented design and describe each technique in outline fashion. Information presented in Chapter 13 may be augmented with material from many of the references contained at the end of the chapter. Because the data flow method has already been presented, it can be used as a "Rosetta Stone"—discussion of the techniques in this chapter can be couched in terms of concepts learned in Chapters 7 and 11, when appropriate parallels exist (in some cases there are none!).

Section 13.3 presents an overview of the Jackson design method. If you use Jackson's book [JAC83] to supplement the material in SEPA, you'll find numerous examples. Many other examples can be found in [CAM89]. You should encourage your students to review Chapter 9 before reading this section.

Section 13.4 presents DSSD, a technique that many call the Warnier-Orr methodology. DSSD is pragmatic and comprehensive, introducing a complete set of notation for representing software requirements and design issues.

In my course in software engineering, I use this as an "F.Y.I. chapter." That is, I expect my students to be familiar with each approach, its basic characteristics and notation, and its underlying strengths and weaknesses. I further expect that each student could represent the solution for a small problem. I do not expect them to be able to apply these techniques to more complex problems. Unless you intend to supplement SEPA extensively, I would suggest that you take the same approach.

PROBLEMS AND POINTS TO PONDER

13.1 Surprisingly, there have not been a large number of papers or studies published that have compared JSD and DSSD (in fact, design methodology comparisons are rare). As a basis for comparison, you might suggest the fundamental analysis and design concepts as criteria. Some of the questions you might ask: (1) how does the method represent the information domain; (2) how is functional partitioning accomplished; (3) how are logical and physical models created; (4) is there an explicit approach to achieving effective modularity; (5) is functional independence achieved; (6) does the method help the design achieve abstraction; (7) information hiding; other design fundamentals; (8) what happens if the data structure is not hierarchical; (9) what special notation or representations distinguish the method; is procedural detail represented and how; (10) what application areas are most amenable to the method?

13.2 As a guide, indicate that the dealer must process the following information:

model
make
year
condition (scale 1 to 10)
wholesale cost
retail cost
options (racing tires, A/C, stereo, etc.)
new/used
days on lot
actual cost (including interest on inventory)
factory incentives

13.3 Before your students attempt to develop a solution using one of the design techniques presented in this chapter, have them develop a paper prototype of this system.

13.4 A comprehensive solution to this problem is contained in Jackson's book [JAC83].

13.5 There is no explicit technique for defining modules in the Jackson Methodology. At the program design level, Jackson moves directly from data organization to a procedural representation. The concept of program structure (although implied) is not explicitly considered.

13.11 Although there aren't too many available references in the literature, you might try:
-    [PET77]
-    Parker, J. "A Comparison of Design Methodologies," *ACM Software Engineering Notes*, October, 1978.
-    Selected papers in *Software Design Techniques* (Freeman and Wasserman, eds.), IEEE.
-    Peters, L. *Software Design*, Yourdon Press, 1981.

Chapter 14
User Interface Design

INTENT

The intent of this chapter is to provide guidance for the design of human-computer interfaces. The chapter begins with a discussion of ergonometric issues, defines the types of human-computer interaction that are common in computer based systems, and provides guidelines for HCI design.

The today's heavy emphasis on graphical user interfaces and the rush toward standardization of these interface, user interface design has become an important issue in systems of all kinds. There was a time when "user friendly" was open to wide interpretation and the design of "good" interfaces was purely an art form. Today, a distinct set of steps can be defined and criteria for assessing the quality of an interface can be established.

Critical Points: Tom understand good HCI design, the student must appreciate the psychological and physiological aspects of human-computer communication. Three different generations of interfaces have evolved, but todays thrust is toward the third generation only. Different models of interfaces can be developed and a design process can be established to create them. Many tools exist to aid in the creation of user interfaces. Design heuristics can be applied to design effective interaction, information display and data input.

CHAPTER OVERVIEW AND COMMENTS

Human perception is a fascinating subject and section 14.1 presents an abbreviated discussion. It is unlikely that you'll have the class time available to consider the topics raised in subsections 14.1.2 and 14.1.3, but you should spend a few moments discussing the four generic tasks listed on p. 460. These tasks must be implemented in an HCI design.

Section 14.2 discusses the three generations of interfaces. You might try to get a video (such as the one available from

Apple) that promote their vision of a fourth generation interface. If time permits, have you student define a next generation interface of their own. What key features (e.g., continuous voice recognition) will be standard?

Section 14.3 defines four different models of a human interface. It is important that your students understand the differences among them. Divide your class into four groups. Describe an application to the entire class and then have each group develop a different model of the user interface for the system. Note differences, discrepancies, etc. In addition, spend a few moments in lecture covering task analysis and compare it to time study techniques conducted by industrial engineers.

The design issues presented in subsection 14.3.3 should be stressed. Ask your students to evaluate these issues for a software package that they are familiar with. Depending on time and your own feeling about emphasis, you might want to expand upon the discussion of UIDS presented in subsection 14.3.4.

Section 14.4 provides a set of checklists for HCI design evaluation. Many of the references for this chapter contain more comprehensive lists.

Interfacing standards (Section 14.5) are a continuing topic of discussion throughout the industry. If you're teaching a graduate class, you might assign each student to research some aspect of one or more interface standards and then present her/his findings in class (this is an extravagant use of time and is recommended for two term courses only).

PROBLEMS AND POINTS TO PONDER

14.1 Your students will have never worked with card input. If you're old enough to remember, describe it too them. Better, use IBM JCL as an example.

14.2 The interface will likely be a WIMP design.

14.4 Command and query interface: To be honest, the negative aspects of this style of interaction make it a poor choice for any application. If pressed, it is appropriate for situations in which an expert user must specify complex sets of highly specific options in a shorthand notation.

Simple menu: is appropriate for situations in which an novice user must specify simple sets of options that can be easily organized in a categorical and hierarchical fashion.

WIMP: There are few situations in which this approach is not best.

14.6 Hypertext can add "three dimensionality" to information retrieval. Instead of a purely hierarchical model of interaction, a Hypertext model enables interaction to be relational. That is, the map for interaction can vary with each user and in each situation.

14.7 through 14.10 If your students have access to prototyping tools (e.g., Macintosh Hypercard) you might have them perform the HCI design tasks, document them and then build an interactive prototype to illustrate their design. Obviously, this is too much to ask if your students are in the middle of a term project. In that case, you might ask them to do the same things for the project on which they are working.

14.11 If response time varies greatly, the user can't develop a rhythm for interaction and frustration results. For example, a user of an editor is deleting text in a document. The sequence of actions is requires a mouse pick on the text to be deleted., followed by either a pull down select on the menu item "delete" or a ^D command sequence. Pick and deletes are underway and a rhythm has been established. The user doesn't even both to check whether the delete has occurred by moves immediately on to the next. A time delay occurs and picks are made before a previous delete has been finalized. The input buffer fills and the user becomes confused when things begin happening that have no relation to the interaction that is currently underway.

Chapter 15
Real-Time Design

INTENT

Effective approaches for the representation and design of real-time systems have improved substantially over the past decade. Although a comprehensive methodology for real-time design is only now evolving, the pieces already exist are are being used in practice. The intent of this chapter is too familiarize the student with the pieces—that is, to provide a basic understanding the the differentiating characteristics of real-time systems and the methods that can be applied to design based on these characteristics.

Throughout this chapter, our focus shifts between design issues associated with systems and those that concentrate on software. Because real-time applications must consider all system elements, a consideration of software alone would be sterile.

Critical Points: The special characteristics of real-time systems provide a unique set of design challenges. Analysis and simulation of real-time systems includes representation and evaluation of performance in a quasi-analytical format. Design techniques for conventional software can be extended to accommodate real-time. Special notation is required to represent the characteristics of real-time software.

CHAPTER OVERVIEW AND COMMENTS

Sections 10.1 and 10.2 provide a reasonably detailed introduction to real-time systems. In general most undergraduate students have not had extensive real-time experience (regardless of their software sophistication). Therefore, lecture supplement (along with appropriate outside readings, if desired) is essential to lay the groundwork for discussions that follow.

If you are conducting a two term software engineering

course, each of the topics presented in section 15.2.n can be given increased emphasis. For example, you might assign an evaluation of your favorite real-time OS and then spend time examining its internals. In fact, this could be coupled with a review of the formal specification of the OS kernel presented in Chapter 9.

Section 15.3 presents an overview of an analysis technique that enables the system or software engineer to determine appropriate timing and sizing information for real-time systems. You might want to provide a bit of queuing theory during lecture so that your students can better appreciate the technique. Subsection 15.3.2 discusses i-Logix Statemate—one of the premier tools for the analysis and simulation of real-time applications. The hierarchical statechart approach, discussed briefly in subsection 15.3.2 is a powerful behavioral modeling notation. If time and emphasis permit, you might want to use [HAR90] as a reference for lecture presentation.

Section 15.4 introduces real-time design methods and delineates the typical problems that are encountered by the designer. Because most real-time design methods represent state transition, the concept of the state transition diagram (or table) should be reviewed in preparation for the sections that follow.

The DARTS design approach is described in section 15.5. DARTS builds on data flow-oriented design methods, but introduces new notation and representation that address real-time issues. You should stress two important extensions that distinguish DARTS—the message communication notation described in Figure 15.10 and the use of communication and synchronization modules as described in Section 15.5.2. I would recommend review of Gomma's papers [GOM84] and [GOM86] prior to the creation of lecture materials.

PROBLEMS AND POINTS TO PONDER

15.1 There are literally hundreds of examples of real-time systems in use today. Among them:
  a. aircraft avionics
  b. simulation systems such as flight trainers
  c. manufacturing process control
  d. medical diagnostic equipment
  e. test monitoring equipment
  f. nearly all embedded military applications

In all situations, the stimuli are always events and information obtained from dynamics real-word activities. In most cases, the system controls hardware.

15.2   This problem should be assigned only if students have had a course in OS and have a basic understanding of OS internals. You might want to spend some lecture time on the key differences between an RTOS and a conventional OS.

15.3   An excellent survey of both Ada and Modula 2 can be found in Wiener and Sincovec's *Software Engineering with Ada and Modula 2*. The reason that real-time language constructs provide advantages is that they tend to decouple the language for the operating system, thereby improving portability.

15.4   The classic example is the producer-consumer problem— see any good book on operating systems for details. This problem might manifest itself when two asynchronous tasks must access the same message buffer; when control software for a two-armed robot must exclude both arms from being in the same place at the same time; when high speed access to a data base by multiple paths must be controlled.

15.5   A reasonably good source of information on queuing theory is Gross and Harris' *Fundamentals of Queuing Theory* (2nd edition).

10.7   See references contained in the **Further Readings** section of SEPA Chapter 22.

Chapter **16**
Programming Languages and Coding

INTENT

Although software design is programming language independent, the choice of a language can influence the efficacy of implementation. In this chapter we consider programming language characteristics that affect the software engineering process. In addition, issues of coding style and coding (design) efficiency are discussed.

Critical Points: Choice of a programming language can affect the ease with which detail design is translated to source code. Modern programming languages are the only practical choice for most software engineering applications. Coding style improves the readability of source code and should be a consideration in all projects.

CHAPTER OVERVIEW AND COMMENTS

As we refine a description (via levels of abstraction) of software a translation process occurs. Section 16.1 describes each step of the translation. You should explain the meaning of "noise"—using examples for each transition—and emphasize the importance (again!) of reviews as a filtering mechanism.

Section 16.2 discusses programming language characteristics and their affect on the software engineering process. Supplementary material for lecture augmentation can be obtained from many of the references at the end of the chapter. Be sure to cover sections 16.2.4 and 16.2.5. Have your students consider choices for languages available in your environment. Is a major language missing, and how does it affect software development?

An overview of programming language fundamentals is presented in section 16.3. Although I don't think significant expansion of this section is necessary in a software engineering course, references such as Pratt's book on programming languages can be invaluable to augment lecture materials.

The language classes defined in section 16.4 were a cause of some debate among the reviewers of this book. Some thought that the classes were too confining, others thought them too broad. You should emphasize that the classes are merely a mechanism that allows us to discuss (albeit briefly) different languages. A parenthetical note: I would recommend against expansion of this topic (I'm certain other courses in your curriculum serve this function)—there are too many other topics that merit attention in software engineering. If however, SEPA is being used in an information systems curriculum with an emphasis on business data processing, you might want to expand discussion of section 16.4.4. Martin's two volume set on 4GLs should provide more than enough information (although be careful about obsolete information).

Section 11.5 provides an overview of coding style. For graduate courses, Kernighan and Plauger [KER78] makes excellent supplementary reading. Ask your students to develop additional guidelines that are consonant with material presented in section 16.5—guidelines may be specific to a local language or programming environment.

The issue of code efficiency is discussed in section 16.6. You should note that many of the efficiency guidelines could be equally well applied to software design. If time permits, it's always interesting to have a "competition" between assembly language and your local high level language:

1. Assign a relatively simple problem.
2. Have students log all development, test and debug time.
3. Measure execution time for both assembly language and HOL.
4. Suggest a non-trivial modification
5. Have students log all time spent on the modification.

Have students draw their own conclusions.

PROBLEMS AND POINTS TO PONDER

16.1   Have your students look for material on "automatic programming" and related topics. Be sure that students address the practical problems that must be solved.

16.2   One of the best sources of information on this topic is the IEEE Tutorial edited by Bill Curtis entitled *Human Factors in Software Development* (2nd edition, 1985). Dozens of reprinted papers are contained in this tutorial. Many other references are noted in Chapter 14.

16.3 and 16.4   You may choose to assign different languages to various students and conduct a short debate. Be sure to note the final question raised in problem 16.4. You might also pose a few different software applications (e.g., an operating system, a video game, a word processing system, an engineering analysis application, etc) and have your students choose the appropriate language, using data derived from these problems as backup.

16.5   Good references for this problem are contained in the Further Readings section at the end of the chapter. Assign a language that is not the development language at your institution.

16.6   Candidate languages might include APL, LISP, SNOBOL or PROLOG. You might choose to assign this problem and problem 16.5 as a single exercise.

16.7   Smalltalk is probably the language of choice here. However, if your institution requires each student to have a PC, you might consider other languages such as Object Pascal, Eiffel or C++.

16.8   Have your students examine which 4GLs are most English-like. Is this necessarily a strong point. This problem can also lead to an interesting lecture discussion on "end-user computing." What are its pros and cons based on other topics presented in this book.

16.9   Refer to your favorite textbook on AI—here are dozens of them!

16.10   The primary distinguishing characteristics of Ada are its packaging concept and its direct support for concurrency, tasking and other real-time oriented features. Ada will be widely used during the early 1990s and will be given increased emphasis at the university level. The language, for all of the controversy that surrounds it, does exhibit excellent software engineering characteristics and is well worth considering in overview fashion during a software engineering course.

16.11 The controversy that surrounds Ada can generally be categorized in three broad areas:

1)   language complexity—some people argue that a language as complex as Ada may be extremely difficult to validate. Given its application in defense systems, this should be a cause for concern.

2)   language application—because the language is complex, some people worry that it will be difficult to learn and therefore will be inappropriately applied—that is, "people will write FORTRAN programs in Ada."

3)   language implementation—Although some progress has been made, Ada compilers remain notoriously slow. Worse, the executable code produced by these compilers is not "tight and fast"—an absolute requirement for embedded software applications.

16.13 to 16.21   Conduct design walkthroughs on resultant programs. Again keep careful logs of errors encountered. Ideally, use a programming language that supports the structured constructs directly, e.g., Ada, Pascal, Modula 2 or C.

Part **IV**

Chapter **17**
Software Quality Assurance

INTENT

In our attempt to understand and apply software engineering technology (i.e., analysis methods, design techniques, testing approaches) we sometimes forget there is a set of procedural—rather than technological—activities that can have a profound impact on the quality of the software. In this chapter, I have attempted to define software quality and the procedures that are necessary to achieve effective software quality assurance (SQA). The primary emphasis is placed on formal technical reviews (FTRs), statistical SQA and metrics.

Critical Points: Software quality can be ascertained within the context of both explicit and implicit software requirements. Explicit requirements are defined in the *Software Requirements Specification* and typically present function and performance that the software must satisfy. Implicit requirements are defined using a number of industry models. Many "measures" of quality have been proposed. The formal technical review is one of the most effective mechanisms for ensuring software quality. Software reliability and safety can be evaluated in a systematic fashion.

CHAPTER OVERVIEW AND COMMENTS

Section 17.1 defines the basic components of software quality. During lecture you should emphasize Figure 17.1 and indicate that many of the "factors" described in the figure are difficult to measure quantitatively. I sometimes have student prioritize these characteristics by assigned a weight to each. The role of SQA is also introduced in this section. Use analogies to the hardware manufacturing world during lecture so that your students are sure to understand the role of SQA.

In my opinion Section 17.2 and 17.3 are among the most important in SEPA. Reviews are the single most effective procedural mechanism for ensuring high quality software. Defect amplification (subsection 17.2.2) and the concept of filters provide a compelling argument for reviews. These ideas should be emphasized. Many professors assign section 17.1 and 17.2 at the beginning of their course in software engineering. I see merit in this and would recommend it. The review checklists presented in subsection 17.3.4 can be used as a "crib sheet" for each project team. Make your students aware of these, even if you don't assign reading in Chapter 17 early in the course.

Section 17.3 presents the logistics associated with formal technical reviews. The checklists contained in section 17.3.4 provide a good point of departure for each of the important reviews that are conducted for a computer based system.

Software quality metrics (Section 17.4) present a (partial) quantitative answer to the question "Is this software any good?" Software quality indices make worthwhile management metrics and should be stressed in a management-oriented course. Halstead's work, although controversial, makes interesting subject matter and may warrant expansion at the graduate level. The McCabe metric is an excellent measure for the assessment of procedural design. I introduce the concept of cyclomatic complexity here and re-introduce it in later discussions of white-box testing in Chapter 18.

A detailed discussion of formal methods (section 17.5) when applied to quality assurance is beyond the scope of SEPA, and frankly, except for graduate offerings, beyond the scope of most "first courses in software engineering." However, an overview of these important topics is beneficial. If your department emphasizes formalism, you may choose to expand upon subsection 17.5.1. If you are teaching a management oriented course, I would strongly recommend discussion of subsection 17.5.2. In fact, you might (given time) introduce some of Deming's and Juran's ideas here.

A discussion of software reliability theory (section 17.6) is best left to a course dedicated to the subject. However, if you are conducting a two term course, you may have time to cover the topic briefly. See the IEEE tutorial by Malaiya and Srima (*Software Reliability Models*, 1991) for additional information. However, subsection 17.6.3 on software safety is a "must" lecture topic. As software becomes pervasive in systems of every type, safety issues become increasingly important. Leveson is the expert in this area and her writings can do must to help in lecture preparation.

Section 17.7 discusses the basic elements of an SQA approach and presents an overview of important standards and SQA activities.

PROBLEMS AND POINTS TO PONDER

17.1 The assessment of a computer program can best be accomplished by considering both technical and management criteria. Technical criteria encompass the design fundamentals discussed in Chapter 10. Management criteria include the completeness and consistency of software documentation, the degree to which a program conforms to requirements and the factors noted in Figure 17.1. Complexity metrics, discussed in this chapter provide a quantitative feel.

17.2 In reality, if we define quality as "conformance to requirements," and requirements are dynamic (keep changing), the definition of quality will be dynamic and an assessment of quality will be difficult.

17.3 Quality focuses on the software's conformance to explicit and implicit requirements. Reliability focuses on the ability of software to function correctly as a function of time or some other quantity. Safety considers the risks associated with failure of a computer-based system that is controlled by software. In most cases an assessment of quality considers many factors that are qualitative in nature. Assessment of reliability and to some extent safety is more quantitative, relying on statistical models of past events that are coupled with software characteristics in an attempt to predict future operation of a program.

17.4 Yes. It is possible for a program to conform to all explicit functional and performance requirements at a given instant, yet have errors that cause degradation that ultimately causes the program to fail.

17.5 Absolutely. Many programs have been patched together or otherwise "kludged up" so that they work, yet these program exhibit very low quality if measured by most of the criteria described in Figure 17.1.

17.6 There is often a natural "tension" that exists between these two groups. The reason is simple: the SQA group takes on the role of the "watch dog," flagging quality problems and highlighting shortcomings in the developed software. It is only normal that this would not be embraced with open arms by the software engineering group. As long as the tension does not degenerate into hostility, there is no problem. It is important to note, however, that a software engineering organization should work to eliminate this tension by encouraging a team approach that has developer and QA people working together toward a common goal—high quality software.

17.7 Institute formal technical reviews. After these are working smoothly, any of a number of SQA activities might be implemented: change control and SCM (see Chapter 21); comprehensive testing methodology (see Chapters 18 and 19); SQA audits of documentation and related software.

17.8 Any countable measure that indicates the factors noted in subsection 17.1.1 are candidates. For example, maintainability as measured by mean-time-to-change; portability as measured by an index that indicates conformance to language standard; complexity as measured by McCabe's metric, and so on.

17.9 Typically, an unprepared reviewer will be reading the product materials while everyone else is conducting the review; will be especially quiet throughout the review; will have made no annotation on product materials; will make only very general comments; will focus solely on one part (the part he/she read) of the product materials. As a review leader, you should ask if the person has had time to prepare. If most reviewers have not prepared, the review should be cancelled and rescheduled.

17.10 Assessing style is tricky and can lead to bad feelings if a reviewer is not careful when he/she makes comments concerning style. If the producer gets the feeling that the reviewer is saying, "Do it like I do," it is likely that some resentment will arise. In general, the review should focus on correctness.

17.12 The literature on software metrics is expanding rapidly.

Use *CACM* and the *IEEE Transactions on Software Engineering* as sources of information. Also recent proceedings of the ICSE and COMPSAC are good sources.

17.16 Use the same references noted for problem 12.12. In addition, the book by Musa et al [MUS87] is the most comprehensive treatment of reliability to date.

17.17 For hardware the MTBF concept is based on statistical error data that occurs due to physical wear in a product. In general, when a failure does occur in hardware, the failed part is replaced with a spare. However, when an error occurs for software, a design change is made to correct it. The change may create side effects that generate other errors. Therefore, the statistical validity of MTBF for software is suspect.

17.18 Classic examples include aircraft avionics systems, control systems for nuclear power plants, software contained in sophisticated medical instrumentation (e.g., CAT scanners or MRI devices) control systems for trains or subway systems; elevator control systems.

Chapter 18
Software Testing Techniques

INTENT

Software testing is often the "stepchild" in the family of software engineering methods. Everyone seems to agree that testing is an important quality assurance activity, yet few industry practitioners (and fewer students) have any meaningful knowledge of effective testing techniques.

The intent of this chapter is to provide an introduction to a family of important white-box and black-box testing techniques, and in so doing, to provide the student with the knowledge to conduct testing in a systematic and successful fashion.

Critical Points: A successful test is one that finds an error. Test cases need not be developed in an ad hoc fashion. Each can be designed using techniques that focus on externally observed software function and information characteristics and internally specified procedural design.

CHAPTER OVERVIEW AND COMMENTS

Section 18.1 identifies the key objectives of software testing and sets the tone for Chapters 18 and 19. It is critically important to dedicate lecture time to the objectives of testing, the flow of activities that we call software testing, and the concepts that underlie black-box and white-box testing.

White box testing focuses on procedural design and is the most rigorous of all testing methods. Section 18.2 justifies the need for white-box testing by examining the nature of software defects.

Basis path testing is the most commonly used white-box technique and is presented in Section 18.3. Flow graph notation is introduced and used as a mechanism to demonstrate how cyclomatic complexity can be determined. You should note for your students that the use of flow graphs is optional—that is, cyclomatic complexity can be determined without them. However, the flow graph does provide a compact graphical notation that can be enormously helpful when basis paths are defined. I have not emphasized the use of graph matrices in SEPA; however, you might want to refer to Beizer [BEI90] and spend a bit more time on them, if you're conducting a graduate course.

Section 18.4 presents techniques that exercise logical control structure. Branch testing, domain testing and BRO testing are all considered. This section also introduces data flow testing, a topic that is beyond the scope of most software engineering courses. Subsection 18.4.3 presents an overview of loop testing. It is important to note that loop testing, basis path testing and the condition testing techniques can be used to complement one another and should be used together to generate comprehensive white-box test cases.

Black-box testing is presented in section 18.5. The concept of an equivalence class (subsection 18.5.1) is difficult for some students. You might want to spend some lecture time providing additional examples. BVA is an extension of equivalence partitioning. Any discussion of cause-effect graphing should emphasize the benefits of the decision table as a useful notation for test case design. Frankly, the actual drawing of the cause-effect graphs is tedious and often unnecessary. The end result (i.e., the decision table) can be extremely useful in the design of test cases.

The testing of real-time systems is a challenge for even the most sophisticated software developers. Section 18.6 introduced a basic strategy for test case design, but does not go into great detail Relatively little has been written on this subject.

Testing tools have evolved rapidly over the past decade and today, there are a number of worthwhile tools on the market. Section 18.7 summarizes the principle categories of testing tools and presents a very brief introduction to some of the tools that have been introduced over the past decade. For further discussion, see Chapter 22.

PROBLEMS AND POINTS TO PONDER

18.1 See Myers [MYE79] for an extremely detailed "solution" to this problem.

18.2 You may elect to distribute the program source code to your students (embedding a few errors purposely).

18.3 In addition to those objectives noted in Section 18.1:
a) a successful test demonstrates compliance with function and performance;
b) a successful test uncovers documentation errors;
c) a successful test uncovers interfacing problems.

18.4 As an alternative, you might suggest that your students apply basis path to one or more of the modules that they have created for their term project.

18.5-18.6 With some extensions, these problems could be assigned as a term project.

18.11 For specific input, an error occurs internally resulting in:
1) improper data placed in a global data area;
2) improper flags that will be tested in a subsequent series of tests;
3) improper hardware control that can only be uncovered during system test; yet "correct" output is produced.

18.12 No, even an exhaustive test (if it were possible) may be unable to uncover performance problems and errors in the specification of the software.

18.14 In this case both input and output "equivalence classes" are considered. For each class, the student should identify boundaries based on numeric ranges, elements of a set, system commands, etc.

18.15 A detailed discussion of this memo can be found in the Spring, 1986 edition of New Engineer magazine. Although a cause-effect graph is not presented, a number of solution algorithms are!

18.17 Both black-box and white-box techniques would be applied. Black-box tests would be designed around the programming language that is to be compiled, that is, a number of small programs would be input and the output object code would be checked for correctness. White box tests would be designed to uncover errors in individual lexical and syntax analysis algorithms and assure that all program paths and loops have been exercised.

Chapter 19
Software Testing Strategies

INTENT

Software testing is a multistep process that must be carefully planned and executed to ensure success. The intent of this chapter is to discuss the strategic aspects of testing. Each of the testing steps—unit test, integration test, validation test, system test and other high-order testing—is discussed in some detail. In addition a brief consideration of debugging techniques is presented.

Critical Points: Software testing is a planned and systematic activity that is a pivotal element of software quality assurance. Testing begins "in the small" and evolves into testing "in the large." Debugging is an activity that occurs as a consequence of successful testing (i.e., testing that uncovers an error).

CHAPTER OVERVIEW AND COMMENTS

An overall strategy for software testing is introduced in Section 19.1. The complementary concepts of V&V are introduced, organizational approaches for testing are considered, and the "testing spiral" is discussed. You should emphasize the spiral—I believe it is a useful metaphor for the software engineering process and the relationship of testing steps to earlier definition and development activities. The completion criteria discussion presented in subsection 19.1.4 can be used to key a lengthy lecture presentation on this subject for graduate courses. See [MUS89] for guidance in preparing lecture materials.

Section 19.2 presents unit testing. It is important to emphasize that white-box techniques introduced in Chapter 18 are most advantageous during this testing step. In addition, be sure the student recognizes that effective unit testing requires the creation of a test environment (Figure 19.6) and that the environment requires effort to develop.

Integration testing is presented in Section 19.3. You should be sure to make the distinction between top-down and bottom-up approaches by discussing their advantages and disadvantages.

Don't be dogmatic about a "pure" top down or bottom up strategy. Rather, emphasize the need for an approach that is tied to a series of tests that (hopefully) uncover module interfacing problems. Be sure to discuss the importance of software drivers and stubs (as well as simulators and other test software), indicating that development of this "overhead" software takes time and can be partially avoided with a well thought out integration strategy. Don't gloss over the need for thorough test planning during this step, even if your students won't have time to complete any test documentation as part of their term projects.

Sections 19.4 and 19.5 might have been entitled "high-order testing." Validation testing is considered in Section 19.4. The key point to emphasize is traceability to requirements. In addition, the importance of alpha and beta testing (in product environments) should be stressed. Section 19.5 presents an overview of the important elements of system testing. Very little literature is available on this subject—therefore, it is difficult to suggest any worthwhile supplementary materials. However, a thorough discussion of the problems associated with "finger pointing," possibly with excerpts from Tracy Kidder's outstanding book, *The Soul of a New Machine*, will provide your students with important insight.

The art of debugging is presented in Section 19.6. To emphasize how luck, intuition and some innate aptitude contribute to successful debugging, conduct the following class experiment:

1. Handout a 30 -50 line module with one or more semantic errors purposely embedded in it.
2. Explain the function of the module and the symptom that the error produces.
3. Conduct a "race" to determine:
    a) error discovery time
    b) proposed correction time
4. Collect timing results for the class; have each student submit his or her proposed correction and the clock time that was required to achieve it.
5. Develop a histogram with response distribution.

It is extremely likely that you find wide variation is the students' ability to debug the problem.

PROBLEMS AND POINTS TO PONDER

19.1   Verification focuses on the correctness of a program by attempting to find errors in function or performance. Validation focuses on "conformance to requirements—a fundamental characteristic of quality.

19.2   The most common problem in the creation of an ITG is getting and keeping good people. In addition, hostility between the ITG and the software engineering group can arise if the interaction between groups is not properly managed. Finally, the ITG may get involved in a project too late—when time is short and a thorough job of test planning and execution cannot be accomplished.

An ITG and an SQA group are not necessarily the same. The ITG focuses solely on testing, while the SQA group considers all aspects of quality assurance (see Chapter 17).

19.3   It is not always possible to conduct thorough unit testing in that the complexity of a test environment to accomplish unit testing (i.e., complicated drivers and stubs) may not justify the benefit. Integration testing is complicated by the scheduled availability of unit tested modules (especially when such modules fall behind schedule). In many cases (especially for embedded systems) validation testing for software cannot be adequately conducted outside of the target hardware configuration. Therefore, validation and system testing are combined.

19.4   If only three test case design methods could be selected during unit test they would be:

1.   basis path testing—it's critically important to ensure that all statements in the program have been exercised.
2.   equivalence partitioning—an effective black box test at the module level.
3.   boundary value analysis—"bugs lurk in corners and congregate at boundaries.

Naturally, good arguments can be made for other combinations of test case design techniques.

19.5   Interface:
1.   Call by name confused with call by number?
2.   Correct indices for all arrays?
3.   Interface between modules developed in different programming languages?
       I/O:
       a. Proper ordering of I/O list?
       b. I/O error traps in place?
       c. Field sizes appropriate for data to be produced?
       Local data structure:
1.   Consistent sizing for global data?
2.   Size error traps in place?
3.   Proper implementation of sophisticated structures?
       Computation:
1.   Improper recursive technique?
2.   Divergent iteration due to algorithm design?
3.   Confused or incorrect (out of order) coefficients?
       Control Flow:
1.   Incorrect logical default for an IF-THEN?
2.   Incorrect processing when all case conditions fail?
3.   Errors for > or < ?

19.6   A single rule covers a multitude of situations: All data moving across software interfaces (both external and internal) should be validated (if possible).

       Advantages: Errors don't "snowball."

       Disadvantages: Does require extra processing time and memory (usually a small price to pay).

19.8   The availability of completed modules can affect the order and strategy for integration. Project status must be known so that integration planning can be accomplished successfully.

19.9   No. If a module has 3 or 4 subordinates that supply data essential to a meaningful evaluation of the module, it may not be possible to conduct a unit test without "clustering" all of the modules as a unit.

19.10   Developer, if customer acceptance test is planned. Both developer and customer (user) if no further tests are contemplated.

Chapter 20
Software Maintenance

INTENT

This chapter presents the third generic phase of the software engineering process—maintenance. Maintenance tasks are defined and the problems, procedures and methods that relate to the maintenance of computer software are discussed. In addition, reverse and re-engineering—hot topics in software engineering—are also considered.

It is important to emphasize to your students that all of SEPA may be viewed as a discussion of maintenance, because all software engineering tasks are reapplied during the maintenance phase. The discussion of maintenance in this chapter focuses primarily on the organizational and procedure requirements necessary to conduct effective maintenance.

Critical Points: Software engineering is the best defense against excessive demands for software maintenance. When maintenance must be conducted, we apply all preceding methods and procedures presented in SEPA. Reverse and re-engineering techniques will assist software engineers in their effort to refurbish the "aging software plant."

CHAPTER OVERVIEW AND COMMENTS

Maintenance activities are defined and discussed in section 20.1. You should note the overall cost of maintenance work as a percentage of all dollars spent on software and emphasize the importance of design for adaptability and enhancement. The key point to be made here is that good design can reduce maintenance effort.

Section 20.2 discusses important issues associated with software maintenance and attempts to delineate problems and associated costs. For graduate level courses, you might assign readings from sources noted in the Further Readings portion of Chapter 20.

Software maintainability is discussed in section 20.3. Although this concept can be "measured" only indirectly, it is important to discuss the factors that control maintenance (subsection 20.3.1) and the potential use of quantitative measures (subsection 20.3.2).

An organizational approach to software maintenance is presented in section 20.4. Material in this section is of particular importance to practitioners but should not be overlooked when a student audience is present.

Section 20.5 presents side effects that can occur when existing software is modified. Augment the presentation in SEPA with examples that illustrate how inadvertent errors can be introduced through seemingly innocent modifications. Problem 20.1, if properly drafted, can help to drive home this point.

Section 20.6 provides a set of guidelines for maintaining "alien" code. This discussion should be juxtaposed with the topics presented in section 20.7

Section 20.7 presents an overview of reverse and re-engineering. If time permits, considerably more emphasis can be placed on these topics. A number of interesting re-engineering algorithms have been proposed (e.g., McCabe uses a variation on cyclomatic complexity and program graphs to define areas of re-engineering opportunity). The literature is still rather sparse in this area, but a good source of additional information is an IEEE tutorial by Robert Arnold, *Software Restructuring* (1986). Other paper appear regularly in the typical journals and magazines.

PROBLEMS AND POINTS TO PONDER

20.1   Nothing emphasizes the difficulty and problems associated with maintenance like doing it. If at all possible, assign this problem!

20.2   There are many methods for selecting candidates for preventive maintenance; however, the following criteria should be generic to all:

1)   priority and importance to user community, measured by number of executions per month;

2)   probability that candidate software will be modified or adapted within a predefined time period;

3)   design measures for current software version (e.g., modularity, cohesion, coupling);

4)   state of software documentation (internal and external)

5)   reliability of software to date;

6)   magnitude (time or cost) of projected changes to software;

7)   availability of personnel who are knowledgeable about the software;

8)   availability of personnel to conduct preventive maintenance.

20.3 Usually, they are. Corrective maintenance should be characterized by testing, debugging and correction—the same tasks that occur during software development.

20.4 Obviously, a machine dependent language presents significant (and sometimes insurmountable) problems when software must be adapted to a new hardware environment. HOL, on the other hand, can ease adaptation if: (1) standard conventions are followed; (2) the target configuration supports the HOL compiler, and (3) software engineered documents exist.

20.5 The only realistic answer is: "that depends." Such costs should be included, but contractual, political, organization and practical reasons sometimes mitigate against their inclusion. [You should discuss this issue in class.]

20.6 It will probably expand due to the longevity of software (if N million dollars are spent, you don't throw it away tomorrow).

20.9 Stated simply the original downward mapping is not necessarily based on a set of repeatable and predictable steps. Therefore, there is no "trail of bread crumbs" that enables us to work backward to develop a complete abstraction at a hight level. Also, these are many possible abstractions that might be used at a high level, therefore, there are many potential backward paths.

20.10 Interactivity introduces the human element. A software engineer working in conjunction with a reverse engineering tool can guide the tool and provide the "intelligence" that is extremely difficult to automate.

20.12 For analysis applications (and others) in which two or more independent algorithms can be developed for a module, a spare parts strategy and/or prototyping is an intriguing possibility.

Chapter 21
Software Configuration Management

INTENT

Although software configuration management (SCM) is often viewed as a clerical activity (beneath the dignity of "real" computer scientists and software engineers), it has as much or more to do with successful software engineering as many state-of-the-art methods. In fact, SCM lies at the heart of the integration issue for CASE and is the kernel function in the much-discussed software repository.

The intent of this chapter is to introduce software configuration management concepts from both a management and technical perspective. Basic definitions are presented, the SCI and baseline concept are discussed and a procedural structure for managing change is suggested. From the technical viewpoint, configuration objects and their relationships are defined, techniques for version control are noted and the concept of the project database (repository) is introduced (to be expanded upon in Chapter 23).

Critical Points: SCM is a procedural framework that controls change throughout the software engineering process. Baselines are established for all SCIs and these represent the objects that are tracked, controlled and managed. SCM tasks include identification, change control and version control, auditing and status accounting (reporting). The project database enables a software engineering to understand the impact of change by understanding the relationships between configuration objects. Because change is an inherent part of software engineering, we must control it or it will control us!

CHAPTER OVERVIEW AND COMMENTS

Section 21.1 introduces the baseline concept and describes how baselines and SCIs are related. A list of SCIs is introduced and an object-oriented viewpoint is considered.

Section 21.2 introduces the SCM process and discusses the key questions associated with SCM. In my courses, I used to spend the majority of lecture time on change control, but today, I spend more time discussing configuration objects and the project database (repository). If your audience has a particular interest in SCM tasks, further reading from Babich (see Further Readings) or Bersoff [BER80] are recommended.

Section 21.3 introduces the identification task and expands upon the concept of configuration objects. If you have the time, you can do a detailed E-R model of the SCIs at this point. It is important to related this discussion back to "where-used/how-used" considerations introduced in Chapter 7 when the requirements (data) dictionary was introduced. The key here is to emphasize the ability to assess the impact of change if relationships are well-defined.

Section 21.4 discusses version control, the methods for represented the evolution of different versions and the relationship between versions, variants and components.

Section 21.5 presents the steps associated with the change control process. Figure 21.7 is particularly important and should be covered in almost all types of courses. It is important to emphasize that the control of change is what protects a large project from chaos. I normally spend a few moments going over the mechanics implied by Figure 21.8 and discussion one or more representative SCM tools that accomplish them.

Sections 21.6 and 21.7 re-introduce the concept of the SQA audit and associated reporting mechanisms as a means for ensuring that changes have been properly done. An very brief discussion of SCM standards is presented in section 21.8.

PROBLEMS AND POINTS TO PONDER

21.1 Because change is a fact of life, it is necessary to recognize that iteration occurs in all paradigms for software engineering. The biggest danger is to assume that the software engineering process will flow sequentially from start to finish with no changes. This just is not realistic!

21.2 We have to establish a point at which we "cut the chord." That is, we must define a point beyond which we will not change something without careful (even formal) evaluation and approval.

21.3 A small project might combine analysis and design modeling into a "Development Specification" that would serve as the first SCI. The source would be the second. It is unlikely that a formal Test Specification would be created, but the suite of test cases would be the third SCI. A User's manual would likely be the fourth SCI and executable versions of the software would be the fifth.

Any change to these baseline SCIs might generate the following questions:

1.   What are the effort and cost required?
2.   How complex is the change and what is the technological risk?
3.   Is the software that is to be changed heavily coupled to other components of the system?
4.   Are the modules to be changed cohesive?
5.   What is likely to happen if the change is not implemented properly?
6.   What is the relative importance of this change as compared to other requested changes?
7.   Who will make the change?
8.   How can we be sure that the change is implemented properly?

21.4 Any book on database design would provide pointer here. [GUP91, SEPA Chapter 23] is an excellent source of information.

21.5 See [GUP91, SEPA Chapter 23]

21.8 Other relationships:
   <mapped from>
   <describes>
   <derived from>
   <uses>
   <model of>
   <created using>
   <identified as>

21.12 An SCM audit focuses on compliance with software engineering standards while an FTR concentrates on uncovering errors associated with function, performance or constraints. The audit has a less technological feel.

Part **V**

Chapter **22**
Computer-Aided
Software Engineering

INTENT

The intent of this chapter is to provide a generic overview of CASE. Because the tool domain is changing so rapidly, I have attempted to write this chapter in a way that will cause it to remain meaningful, even after this generation of CASE tools is obsolete.

The chapter begins with a brief discussion of the history of software tools and the overall philosophy of CASE, and a discussion of the overall CASE building blocks. The majority of the chapter is dedicated to a definition and explication of a CASE tools taxonomy.

Critical Points: CASE is similar in many ways to CAD/CAE/CIM for engineering in other disciplines. CASE building blocks create an environment architecture that forms the basis of integration (Chapter 23). The taxonomy of tools spans the entire software engineering process, covering methods and procedures support and umbrella activities (e.g., SCM).

CHAPTER OVERVIEW AND COMMENTS

The chapter begins with a trip back in time in section 22.1. If you are familiar with the evolution of CAD/CAE/CIM tools, it is both interesting and important to discuss the CASE parallels for software engineering. It is equally important to indicate where the analogy breaks down and (depending upon the sophistication of your students), discussing the impact of CASE on technical cultures for software development (see Pressman, R., *Making Software Engineering Happen*, Prentice-Hall, 1988 for additional information).

Section 22.1 discusses the building blocks that are required to construct a CASE environment. The presentation here is meant to lay the foundation for more detailed discussion in Chapter 23.

The CASE tools taxonomy is introduced in section 22.3. Note the caveats that I mention in the text. Any taxonomy is open to criticism and I encourage you to present alternatives to your students, if you feel that a different categorization would be more meaningful or appropriate. Note also, that the Further Readings section at the end of the chapter contains a table that lists representative tools for each of the tool classes and sub-classes presented in sections 22.4 through 22.13.

You can use the remaining sections of this chapter in one of two ways. The material can be presented sequentially when this chapter is covered in class, or relevant sections can be assigned earlier in a software engineering course as the method or topic to which the tool class applies is being covered.

Section 22.4 introduces business system planning tool. I give these very short shrift in SEPA for one important reason: they are rarely used by software engineers, rather, they are applied by consultants who have been hired to evaluate the information system requirements of an entire organization. If you want to stress these tools, I recommend [MAR89] for additional information.

Section 22.5 presents a number of different types of project management tools. I would strongly recommend coverage of this section if you are teaching a management oriented course. It can be assigned along with readings in SEPA Chapters 2, 3 and 4.

Section 22.6 cover support tools—a potpourri category that combines network communication tools, SCM tools and documentation tools under one roof.

Analysis and design tools are presented in section 22.7 and are relevant to many of the topics presented in SEPA Parts II and III. Since tools in this class will evolve rapidly, you should do some research of your own and attempt to present the current state of the art in this area when you teach the course. It is likely that analysis and design engines (subsection 22.7.4 will become quite sophisticated and may be an interesting topic for discussion. If you've taken advantage of the *Software Engineering Teaching System*, you'll be able to demonstrate some of these tools, rather than just talk about them!

Section 22.8 describes programming tools. In this context, the term programming refers to activities associated with the direct creation and manipulation of source code. I do not spend much time on 4GLs in SEPA because most courses do not emphasize this topic. If you intent to emphasize 4GT and 4GLs and the tools that support them, you'll need supplementary readings for this section.

Subsection 22.8.3 focuses on object-oriented programming tools. I would suggest that you spend lecture time discussing the "browser" as a tool and more importantly, the notion of classification of program components. As I indicated earlier, the classification problem is the focus of substantial research (see *CACM*, January, 1991).

Section 22.9 presents an overview of different types of testing tools. If you spend time discussing these tools, you should relate the discussion to topics presented in Chapters 18 and 19.

As noted in the text for section 22.10, prototyping tools span a broad gamut of tool types. You should emphasize that the trend today is toward prototypers that ultimately lead to production code.

Tools for reverse and re-engineering (section 22.11) are one of the hottest of all CASE areas. An increasing number of these tools (some with new and sophisticated features) will emerge as we move into the mid-1990s. I would recommend that you research this area and present your students with an updated view of the reverse/re-engineering tool set. It will likely have changed substantially since SEPA was published.

Framework tools (section 22.12) tie it all together. At the time of this writing, the framework domain is in flux. You should discuss this section after having your students read Chapter 23.

The potential for AI and CASE (section 22.13) is high (but then again, the *potential* for AI and just about everything is high!!). I do not believe that AI will have substantial impact in the CASE arena in the short term. However, it is possible that *real* AI-based CASE tools (many vendors make claims about AI that are pure marketing hype) will begin to emerge late in the 1990s.

PROBLEMS AND POINTS TO PONDER

22.1 Even thought a student list may be short, you should insist that students consider the tool box that they apply to "write programs." For industry practitioners: the list can number dozens of tools—some used globally and some used local to one group. Try to categorize.

22.2 The answer is yes.
CAD/CAM:

1965:	rudimentary CAD drawing tools
1970:	the first CAE elements and more sophisticated drawing tools
1975:	integration (albeit limited) with CAM
1980:	more sophisticated CAD/CAE and CAM integration
1985:	advances such as solid modeling; simulation; design engines and tool integration

CASE:

1975:	rudimentary tools, compilers, editors
1980:	first drawing tools for analysis and design
1985:	integration (albeit limited) with code generators
1990:	more sophisticated CASE with first steps toward tool integration
1995: (?)	advances such as ...

22.3 The only real strength of the mainframe based development environment is the ability to concentrate all information in one location (although a software engineering data base was rarely if ever created).

22.4 The key here is information hiding and decoupling. That is, the portability services should be designed in a way that hides operation system details from the CASE environment and decouples and CASE related tools from the OS.

22.5 Many options exist:
• management tools and technical tools
• front end tool (sometimes call "upper case") and back-end tools (sometimes called "lower case")
• development tools, control tools and management tools
among others.

22.6 The question to ask yourself is: does this tool serve sole to plan, control or track a software project? If so, it's a management tool. If the tool is used to create models of software, source code itself, or to exercise the program that is created, it is a technical tool. Umbrella tools, apply throughout the software engineering process and would include certain management tools, SCM tools, framework tools, etc.

22.13 There are many situations in which dynamic analysis tools for software testing are "the only way to go." For example, if an embedded application is to be build and performance of various software functions is crucially important, a dynamic tool can provide an important window into the system operation. Another situation: an interactive system is to build and heavy testing of the interface is mandatory. In addition, it is likely that many changes to the system will occur over the first year of operation, demanding heavy regression testing with each change. A capture/playback tool can reduce the effort required to conduct regression tests by a substantial percentage.

Chapter 23
Integrating CASE Environments

INTENT

CASE tools provide benefits, even when they are used as a "point solution" to a specific software engineering procedure or method. But the real benefit of CASE lies in the integration of individual tools to form an environment. The intent of this chapter is consider the current status of integrated CASE (I-CASE).

Fundamental integration requirements and existing integration options are presented early in the chapter. With these basics out of the way, a generic architectural model for CASE tools integration is discussed. Finally, the impact of the CASE repository—one of the hottest topics in software engineering—is considered and proposed integration standards are discussed.

Critical Points: Integration is the real power behind CASE, yet the requirements for an I-CASE environment are not easy to achieve. Many different modes of integration exist. The architecture for full integration encompasses a number of different layers that allow integration of interfaces, tools, data and hardware and software. The CASE repository, also called a project database in Chapter 21, can be modeled as a collection of interrelated objects.

CHAPTER OVERVIEW AND COMMENTS

Integration is achieved when programs, documents and data (and fragments of each of these) can be smoothly passed from tool to tool in an I-CASE environment. In section 23.1 the requirements for CASE integration are discussed. You might decide to spend additional time discussing the "integration framework" proposed by a specific vendor. *Software Magazine* discusses (in a typically superficial fashion) each vendor framework offering in the March, 1991 (vol. 11, no. 4) edition.

Section 23.2 presents each of the integration options that is available to software engineering organizations. You should stress the fact that most developers currently use point solutions or simple data exchange, but that the wave of the future is full integration.

Section 23.3 defines an architectural model (see Figure 23.3) for full integration. If time permits, you might want to spend time discussion options for creating the user interface layer relative to the many interface standards and tool kits that are available today.

The mechanisms that enable tool integration are discussed in section 23.4 The "trigger" concept may be difficult for some student to grasp (see Problem 23.3). You should indicate that trigger can be automatically invoked, but they can also be activated via commands that occur at the interface.

Section 23.5 consider the modes of integration among tools and between tools and data. In essence, data-tool integration encapsulates (in an object-oriented sense) configuration items and the tools (functions) that operate on them. Data-data integration is analogous to a data modeling activity, in which objects and their relationships are defined.

The CASE repository is introduced in section 23.6. The functions performed in conjunction with the repository (subsection 23.6.1) should be discussed in detail. Again, *Software Magazine* (March, 1991) may be of use if you intend to discuss vendor implementation of these functions. Repository content and the use of metadata (subsection 23.6.2) can be the catalyst for a detailed discussion of object-oriented databases or the implementation of an object-oriented view using a relational model. You might also revisit or expand upon discussions of version control and SCM originally presented in Chapter 21. Unless you have a specific reason for doing so, I would not recommend spending the time presenting repository and integration standards in any detail.

PROBLEMS AND POINTS TO PONDER

23.1 An example the jumps to mind is medical instrumentation and information management. But collecting, collating, relating and reporting the results from many tests on the same patient, a doctor has a better chance of deriving an accurate diagnosis.

Another example is automated manufacturing. Machines and manufacturing cells are integrated so that materials flow more smoothly among them.

23.3 Using jargon that was introduced earlier in this book, a "trigger" is an event that causes the CASE environment to change state. For example, once a particular configuration item has been created, the sequential flow of software engineering events may dictate that another technical activity (and associated tool) be applied to the information that was produced. A trigger is generated by the first tool and causes a second tool to be invoked to operate on data that was produced by the first tool. Alternatively, a trigger can be invoked by a software engineer during his or her interaction with the I-CASE environment interface.

23.5 There are considerably more similarities than difference is the mechanisms noted. Both enable processes to be initiated, both allow for interprocess (tool) communication, both allow basic data elements (objects) to be manipulated, both allow information to be shared across a distributed network environment. The primary difference between operating system mechanisms and CASE environment mechanisms is in focus, not function. The OS mechanisms sit "behind" the CASE mechanisms, often providing the machine dependent features that enable them to perform their function.

23.7 In essence, data-tool integration encapsulates (in an object-oriented sense) configuration items and the tools (functions) that operate on them.

23.8 Metamodel and metadata are terms that describe a model or data that are used to describe a model or data. For example, metadata is used to describe the attributes of a configuration item such as a design specification. The generic contents of the specification are described with metadata. The information contained within the specification is data.

23.10 Requirements tracing might be implemented using a CASE tool that extracts requirements from an RFP (see Chapter 22). Once requirements have been codified and entered in the repository. Each SCI is related to one or more requirements. With these relationships established, the repository can be queries to determine which SCIs satisfy which requirements.

Chapter **24**
The Road Ahead

INTENT

The intent of this chapter is to provide a peek into the future of software engineering practice. Like any attempt at crystal ball gazing, my projections may be off the mark, but the general trends outlined in this final chapter of SEPA are highly likely to emerge as the 1990s progress.

The scope of change in software engineering technology is characterized in terms of the 5-5-5 rule. Changes and their affect on people, the process, the product (information) and the discipline (software engineering are discussed.

Critical Points: Software engineering in the late 1990s will be different from the discipline that we know today, but not as different as some people believe. The human-computer environment for software engineering may experience the most profound changes. The process will evolve slowly, moving toward an evolutionary paradigm. Tools and software itself will target the creation of knowledge as well as information [the distinction (described in section 24.5) is important]. Technology (both hardware and software) will continue to be a primary driver.

CHAPTER OVERVIEW AND COMMENTS

Section 24.1 revisits the importance of computer software. The key aspect of this discussion is "software as differentiator." It is interesting to have your students come up with examples of software as a differentiator for products and services.

The 5-5-5 rule (section 24.2) seems to be a reasonable model for technologies in the last quarter of this century. Have your students do a bit of research on the history of one or more important technologies and see if they fit into the 5-5-5 progression.

People and cultures change very slowly. In section 24.3, I make the argument that and evolving software engineering environment may have as much or more to do with people issues (in software engineering) that the people themselves. As tools, interaction mechanisms, and methodology mature, the culture for building software may change accordingly.

Evolutionary models for software engineering (section 24.4) are the most likely candidates for prominence in the mid and late 1990s. Discuss the difference between the evolutionary view espoused by the spiral model and the sequential view suggested by the classic life cycle. Refer to chapter 1 for the pros and cons of these paradigms.

In section 24.5, the new role of software as a knowledge processor is discussed. Ask your students to come up with two or three additional analogies similar to the one presented on p. 769 of SEPA. If time permits, you might want to take a brief foray into the current status of AI software.

The technology evolution of both hardware and software is presented in section 24.6. You should update Figures 24.4 and 24.5 as appropriate. [HOP90] make for interesting reading. If you're teaching a graduate course, you might want to assign it.

PROBLEMS AND POINTS TO PONDER

24.1 *The Wall Street Journal* is an excellent source of article of this type. This week: *Newsweek* talked about the importance of software in reducing automobile emissions, *Business Week* talked about the future of Microsoft as a software power, and *Time* discussed the use of telephone call identification and databases and their impact on personal privacy.

24.5 As this is being written, the hostilities in the Gulf War have come to a close. Regardless of your political point of view, I believe an excellent case study would be to move from data about the war to information synthesized from the data, to knowledge about war in remote theaters of operation to "wisdom" about the role of the U.S. in the global world order. Try it ... you might come up with something interesting!

AFTERTHOUGHTS

When you write a reasonably successful book and are asked to begin a yet another edition, the first thought that crosses your mind is, "Good, now I can fix all the shortcomings of the preceding edition, respond to the many, many suggestions proposed by adopters, and re-establish SEPA as the most widely used textbook on software engineering—I'll make this book a lot better!"

Once all the research, writing, editing and iteration are complete, you look back on what you've done and hope that the result is "a lot better." But you're never completely satisfied. There are additional topics you wish were included, expanded discussion that could provide benefit, last minute insights that occur while reading page proofs, and a multitude of additional sins. The above comments not withstanding, I sincerely hope that *Software Engineering: A Practitioner's Approach* provides you with an effective foundation for teaching software engineering.

As always, I welcome your comments, your corrections, and your criticism and wish you the best of luck in applying my book.

RSP

YOUR NOTES

APPENDIX I
SOFTWARE ENGINEERING BIBLIOGRAPHY

Version 8.2
copyright © 1992
R.S. Pressman & Associates, Inc.
(reproduced with permission)

As part of our service to clients, RSP&A has developed an annotated list of books that should be made available in any library that desires a well-rounded collection in software engineering. We recommend that you use these as a comprehensive source of information on software engineering. The annotated list is organized in the following manner:

> Software Engineering Management
>> General Interest
>> Metrics and Productivity Issues
>> Project Management
>> Technology Transition
>> People Management
>> Legal Issues
> Software Engineering Technology
>> Full Coverage Textbooks
>> Systems Engineering: Hardware and Software
>> Analysis and Specification
>> Formal Methods
>> Software Design
>>> Conventional Methods
>>> User Interfaces
>>> Object-Oriented Methods
>>> Fundamental Topics
>>> Real-Time Software Design
>> Quality Assurance and Testing
>> Software Maintenance
>> Tools, Environments, CASE and Other Topics
> Software Engineering: Other Information Sources

To help you get started, I have identified especially valuable books with the symbol, Δ, after the bibliography entry.

SOFTWARE ENGINEERING MANAGEMENT

General Interest

Δ Crosby, P., **Quality Is Free, McGraw-Hill, 1979.**

This book describes how to manage quality so that it becomes a source of profit. Not specifically directed at software, the book nonetheless provides excellent insight into quality issues associated with software. To quote Business Week: " The executive who spends half the day digesting this book may find it one of the most valuable investments of time he or she has made."

Feigenbaum, E.A., and P. McCorduck, The Fifth Generation, Addison-Wesley, 1983.

A New York Times best seller that describes (in what some have criticized as overly dramatic terms) the impact of artificial intelligence and expert systems and the business implications of knowledge engineering. The economic "threat" posed by Japanese efforts in this area is examined.

Kidder, T., The Soul of a New Machine, Little, Brown & Co., 1981.

This Pulitzer prize winning, non-fiction best seller chronicles the development of a state-of-the-art computer system. It provides good insight into the psyche of both hardware and software engineers and introduces the reader to technical concepts in a painless fashion. Note: Many of the practices described in the book are not recommended in a well-controlled software engineering environment.

Stoll, C., The Cuckoo's Egg, Doubleday, 1989.

A New York Times best-seller that describes the world of computer networks and the invasion of hackers. Non-fiction, but written like a high tech detective novel, this book makes interesting reading for anyone interests in computer security.

Toeffler, A., Powershift, Bantam, 1990.

A New York Times bestseller, Toeffler completes a trilogy that included *Future Shock* and *The Third Wave*. In this book, he contends that computers and software are creating a shift in the worlds power structures, Fascinating reading by a master futurist.

Metrics and Productivity Issues

Arthur, L.J., Measuring Programmer Productivity and Software Quality, Wiley, 1985.

A somewhat superficial, but still useful, survey of software metrics. Presents measures of the software development process and technical measures of software. Considers both quantitative and qualitative measures.

Arthur, L.J., Programmer Productivity, Wiley, 1983.

An extremely readable treatment of software productivity, this book presents a good qualitative overview of the topic. Presents a concise description of function points and their impact on productivity measurement.

Dreger, J. B., Function Point Analysis, Prentice-Hall, 1989.

The first book dedicated to function point analysis, the metrics approach that is preferred by many software development organizations. Provides a solid tutorial that indicates how to compute function points and how to use them.

Δ Grady, R.B. and D.L. Caswell, Software Metrics: Establishing a Company-Wide Program, Prentice-Hall, 1987.

An excellent book describing Hewlett-Packard's efforts to institute a software metrics program. Must reading for anyone who is contemplating a similar endeavor.

Jones, T.C. (ed.), Programming Productivity: Issues for the Eighties, IEEE Computer Society Press, 1981.

This book is an anthology of important papers that address software "productivity" and quality. Methods for measurement of productivity, life cycle analysis, methodologies, and programming environments are considered. The reader can pick and choose from among many topics.

Δ Jones, T.C., Programming Productivity, McGraw-Hill, 1986.

In this significant extension of his original anthology, Jones presents an in depth discussion of methods for measuring, interpreting and improving software engineering productivity and quality. A thorough and pragmatic treatment of the subject.

Parikh, G., Programmer Productivity, Reston, Publishing, 1984.

Still another of a growing number of texts on this subject. The author presents a useful (although somewhat superficial) survey of "productivity methods, tools and procedures."

Project Management

Δ Babich, W.A., Software Configuration Management, Addison-Wesley, 1986.

An abbreviated, yet effective, treatment of pragmatic issues in software configuration management. More readable and current than Bersoff et al., this book covers all important SCM tasks and surveys existing tools.

Bell, P. and C. Evans, Mastering Documentation, Wiley, 1989.

This book contains outlines for all important documents as well as many useful guidelines for writing specifications, user guides, etc.

Bersoff, E., V. Henderson and S. Siegal, Software Configuration Management, Prentice-Hall, 1980.

This book is one of the few that focuses on software configuration management. Although the treatment is somewhat general, a number of excellent case studies are presented; good overall guidelines are proposed, and key terminology and concepts are introduced.

Boddie, J., *Crunch Mode*, Prentice-Hall, 1987.

Recommended reading for all managers who "have 90 days to do a six month project." This little book focuses on the real life compromises that occur when time pressure overrides all else.

Δ Boehm, B., Software Engineering Economics, Prentice Hall, 1981.

Written by the director of software development for TRW, this book presents a comprehensive treatment of software estimating, project planning and control. Somewhat mathematical and technical in parts, the text introduces Boehm's COCOMO estimation modeling scheme and provides useful data on software development productivity.

Δ Boehm, B., Risk Management, IEEE Computer Society Press, 1989.

An excellent tutorial on risk analysis and management, this book contains many excellent papers on risk and related topics as well as Boehm's notes on the subject. Presents a number of worthwhile checklists, forms and guidelines for managing risk.

Δ Brooks, F., The Mythical Man-Month, Addison-Wesley, 1975.

This classic text, written by a manager of one of IBM's largest software development efforts, depicts many of the problems (and some of the solutions) associated with software. The book is written in an informal, sometimes humorous style. Anecdotes abound.

Case, A.F., Information Systems Development: Principles of Software Engineering and CASE, Prentice-Hall, 1986.

This book is one of the first to emphasize the use of Computer-Aided Software Engineering (CASE) as an approach to information systems development. Emphasizes management issues and presents an overview of important techniques. Contains useful guidelines for the implementation of software engineering and CASE.

Δ **Charette, R., Software Engineering Risk Analysis and Management, McGraw-Hill, 1989.**

One of the first books dedicated to risk assessment and its role in the management of software projects. Topics covered include risk identification, estimation, evaluation, and control.

DeGrace, P and L. Hulet-Stahl, Wicked Problems, Righteous Solutions, Yourdon Press, 1990.

A worthwhile survey of software engineering paradigms and their strengths and weaknesses.

Δ **DeMarco, T., Controlling Software Projects, Yourdon Press, 1982.**

A thorough and pragmatic treatment of all important aspects of software management. Excellent sections on project metrics and a useful discussion of software quality issues.

Frank, W.L., Critical Issues in Software, Wiley, 1983.

This book provides a current and practical guide to software economics, strategy and profitability. Useful statistics and case studies abound. Contains a comprehensive bibliography.

Freeman, P., Software Perspectives, Addison-Wesley, 1987.

This book considers software engineering from a a unique system perspective. Freeman discusses the major components of the software engineering process in a style that is particularly well suited to managers.

Δ **Gilb, T., Principles of Software Engineering Management, Addison-Wesley, 1988.**

A thought-provoking discussion of software engineering and its management by an industry iconoclast and respected consultant. Gilb discusses everything from scheduling to risk assessment, from walkthroughs to motivation of staff. An interesting read.

Glass, R., Software Conflict, Yourdon Press, 1991.

A short collection of essays on software engineering. Procedures, methods and tools are each considered in a style that is often humorous, sometime irreverent and always thought-provoking.

Gunther, R.C., Management Methodology for Software Product Engineering, Wiley, 1978.

This book provides excellent guidance for managers who must plan and control products in which software is a critical (but not the only) element. The concept of "software as a product" is introduced and the management disciplines to control product planning, development, services, documentation, support, testing, and maintenance are discussed. A number of interesting case studies, guidelines and outlines are included.

Δ **Leveson, N., Software Safety, Prentice-Hall, 1989.**

This book presents essential information required to assess the technology risks associated with computer-based systems. Leveson is the recognized expert on the subject and her book is one of the few available to the industry.

Londiex, B., Cost Estimation for Software Development, Addison-Wesley, 1987.

The is contains a detailed presentation of the Putnam estimation model, with consideration of other models for comparison. Its strength lies in many useful examples.

Ould, M.A., Strategies for Software Engineering, Wiley, 1990.

Discusses management decision making in the context of software projects with an emphasis on risk reduction and product quality.

Page-Jones, M., Practical Project Management, Dorset House Publishing, New York, 1985.

A good introduction to information systems project management. Presents basic elements of estimation, planning and scheduling, project tracking, team organization and other management topics. Must be supplemented with other texts for detailed study.

Δ   **Pressman, R.S., Software Engineering: A Practitioner's Approach, 3rd edition, McGraw-Hill, 1992.**

This best-selling book presents a thorough treatment of software engineering and includes both management and technical topics. Recommended for those who need an understanding of each step in the software engineering process. Contains an extensive bibliography.

Δ **Pressman R. S. and S.R. Herron, Software Shock, Dorset House, 1991.**

A book on software that is directed toward the non-technical professional. The people, the process, the tools, the problems and the opportunities are each covered. Makes excellent reading for senior managers and others who must understand the danger and opportunity offered by software.

Reifer, D.J. (ed.), Software Management, IEEE Computer Society Press, 2nd edition, 1981.

This book is an anthology of important papers on software management. Topics include: planning, organizing, staffing, directing, and controlling software projects. A number of case studies are presented.

Roetzheim, W.H., Developing Software to Government Standards, Prentice-Hall, 1991.

One of the few books that is dedicated to a discussion of software development under DoD-STD 2167A. An good overview of important topics prior to wading into the voluminous government standards.

Simpson, W.D., New Techniques in Software Project Management, Wiley, 1987.

A good overview of software project management, this book provides useful information for the new manager. The author emphasizes team management.

Whitten, N., Managing Software Development Projects, Wiley, 1989.

An introduction for new managers and those that need to understand the important issues associated with software project management.

Youl, D.P., Making Software Development Visible, Wiley, 1990.

This small book emphasizes project tracking—a topic that is often given short shrift in other software project management texts.

People Management

Cougar, J.D., and R.A. Zawacki, Motivating and Managing Computer Personnel, Wiley-Interscience, 1980.

This book is a comprehensive view of "human resource management" for companies involved in the development of computer based systems. The authors suggest methods, based on findings culled from a large industry study, that help reduce employee turnover, improve work quality and motivate professional development.

Δ **DeMarco, T. and T. Lister, Peopleware, Dorset House, 1987.**

This book considers the management of the most important software development resource—people. Writing style is light and anecdotal, but the message is an important one. The authors present particularly useful discussions of office layout, "productivity," hiring the right software people, and team building.

House, R.H., The Human Side of Project Management, Addison-Wesley, 1988.

Takes a psychological/behavioral view of the management of large technical projects. A pragmatic treatment that focuses on an area of management that is often neglected.

Licker, P.S., The Art of Managing Software Development People, Wiley, 1985.

This book presents a somewhat academic but still useful treatment of the subject. The author considers typical management problems and their solutions, human resources management and training of new managers in the software development world.

Δ **Weinberg, G.M., Becoming a Technical Leader, Dorset House, 1986.**

This book is *must* reading for all technical managers and any technical person who aspires to a management or technical leadership position. Written in an entertaining style filled with anecdotes, self-tests and challenging ideas, Weinberg's book will likely become a classic. The author presents important models for leadership style, innovation and motivation that benefit every reader.

Weinberg, G.M., Understanding the Professional Programmer, Dorset House, 1988. Δ

This collection of essays provides an intriguing look into the "head" of software engineers. Filled with amusing anecdotes and useful insight this book will help managers better understand their people.

Technology Transition

Bouldin, B.M., Agents of Change, Yourdon Press, 1989.

Provides guidance for managing technological change within a software development organization. A good companion text to Pressman, R.S., *Making Software Engineering Happen.*

Buckley, F.J., Implementing Software Engineering Practice, Wiley, 1989.

Presents a reasonable overview of management topics in software engineering and provides simple guidelines for implementing the technology.

Δ **Humphrey, W.S., Managing the Software Process, Addison-Wesley, 1989.**

Introduces a software process maturity model (developed at the SEI) that is very useful for assessing the status of software engineering practice within an organization. Presents many management topics in the context of the process maturity model.

Δ **Pressman, R.S., Making Software Engineering Happen, Prentice-Hall, 1988.**

The first book to treat the problems associated with the installation of software engineering practice. Defines a "life cycle" for software engineering implementation that includes assessment, education, selection, installation and evaluation. Provides practical, proven methods for making the transition to software engineering practice.

Legal Issues

Auer, J., and C.E. Harris, *Computer Contract Negotiations,* **Van Nostrand-Reinhold, 1981.**

Presents useful guidelines for negotiating hardware and software contracts. Includes checklists and contract formats.

Gemignani, M., Law and the Computer, CBI Publishing, Boston, 1981.

This book provides a useful overview of legal issues associated with computer based systems. Topics include: an introduction to legal concepts and terminology, legal protection of software, liability, contracts and other issues.

Harris, T.D., The Legal Guide to Computer Software Protection, Prentice-Hall, 1985.

Focusing solely on software, this guide provides useful, up-to-date information on copyrights, patents, trademarks, software publishing and trade secrets. Written for the layman.

Knight, P. and J. Fitzsimons, The Legal Environment of Computing, Addison-Wesley, 1990.

With chapters on copyright, patents, privacy, contracts, negligence, anti-trust and other topics, this book provides a useful overview of computing and software legal issues for the non-lawyer.

SOFTWARE ENGINEERING TECHNOLOGY

Full Coverage Textbooks

The following books cover most or all aspects of software engineering. In most cases the topic is presented by considering various steps in the software engineering process.

Fairley, R., Software Engineering Concepts, McGraw-Hill, 1985.

A life cycle treatment of the software engineering process. Presents a worthwhile overview of important aspects of the technology. Contains a good bibliography.

DeMarco, T. and T. Lister, Software State-of-the-Art, Dorset House, 1990.

A comprehensive anthology of important papers published in the field over the past 20 years.

Ince, D., Software Engineering, VanNostrand Reinhold, 1990.

An abbreviated treatment that could serve as an overview to the subject.

Lamb, D.A., Software Engineering: Planning for Change, Prentice-Hall, 1988.

A concise treatment of software engineering that touches on each of the important steps in the process. Goods example documents are contained in an appendix.

Ledgard, H., Software Engineering Concepts (vol. 1) and Programming Practice (vol. 2), Addison-Wesley, 1987.

This two volume set presents a concise treatment of software engineering. Contains useful discussions of team approaches, human factors as a software design criteria and elements of programming style.

Macro, A. and J. Buxton, The Craft of Software Engineering, Addison-Wesley, 1987.

This up-to-date survey of software engineering discipline covers most important aspects of the "craft." Although a bit superficial in places (particularly design), the book contains an interesting case study that illustrates important software engineering principles.

Ng, P. and Yeh, R.T., Modern Software Engineering, VanNostrand Reinhold, 1990.

A full coverage text book with specific emphasis on research topics and directions. Contains worthwhile chapters on analysis and design as well as coverage of specialized topics.

Pressman, R.S., Software Engineering: A Beginner's Guide, McGraw-Hill, 1988.

This book is intended to introduce software engineering at an introductory level. Designed for use in introductory college courses, the book contains a step-by-step "cook book" for software engineering practice.

Δ **Pressman, R.S., Software Engineering: A Practitioner's Approach, 2nd edition, McGraw-Hill, 1987.**

The most widely used textbook in software engineering. Covers all steps in the software engineering process, presenting in-depth treatment of important project management, analysis, design, coding and testing methods as well as "umbrella activities" such as SQA, SCM, and reviews.

Shooman, M., Software Engineering, McGraw-Hill, 1983.

A overview of all steps of the life cycle; in-depth discussion of software reliability issues.

Software Engineering Handbook, McGraw-Hill, 1986.

Originally developed by the General Electric Company for internal use, this handbook can serve as a foundation for developing local software engineering guidelines. Discussions of the technology are somewhat dated, but the Handbook contains a a good "comprehensive example" and a thorough discussion of documentation format, content and organization.

Δ **Sommerville, I., Software Engineering, 3rd edition, Addison-Wesley, 1989.**

An in-depth treatment of software engineering that treats most important topics thoroughly and clearly. Expanded treatment in third edition considers object-oriented techniques, the design of user interfaces and other current topics.

Vick, C.R., and C. Ramamoorthy (eds.), Handbook of Software Engineering, Van Nostrand-Reinhold, 1984.

An encyclopedic discussion of wide-ranging topics related to software and computer-based systems development. An excellent reference source.

Weiner, R. and R. Sincovec, Software Engineering with Modula-2 and Ada, Wiley, 1984.

A reasonably complete treatment of software engineering. The primary importance of this book is its use of Modula-2 and Ada, two important and relatively new programming languages, to illustrate important concepts.

Systems Engineering: Hardware and Software

Athey, T., Systematic Systems Approach, Prentice-Hall, 1982.

Presents an integrated method for solving systems problems. Stresses quantitative analysis techniques.

Blanchard, B.S., and W. Fabrycky, Systems Engineering and Analysis, Prentice-Hall, 1981.

A detailed treatment of all aspects of systems engineering. Includes analytical engineering techniques.

Thayer, R.H. and M. Dorfman, System and Software Requirements Engineering, IEEE Computer Society Press, 1990

A voluminous tutorial on system and software requirements analysis. Contains reprints of over 30 papers on methods, tools and management issues.

Analysis & Specification

Boar, B.H., Application Prototyping, Wiley, 1985.

A discussion of prototyping in a data processing environment. Contains good arguments for prototyping as an alternative to conventional specification.

Braithwaite, K., Analysis, Design & Implementation of Data Dictionaries, McGraw-Hill, 1988.

One of the few texts that is dedicated to data dictionaries, this book presents an extremely thorough treatment of the subject. Data dictionary concepts, design and examples in various application areas are presented. However, treatment of CASE implementations is weak.

Davis, A.M., Software Requirements Analysis and Specification, Prentice-Hall, 1990.

A full coverage textbook on analysis and specification methods and tools. Distinguished by a comprehensive bibliography containing well over 100 references to recent work in this area.

Δ **DeMarco, T., Structured Analysis and System Specification, Prentice-Hall, 1979.**

A definitive treatment of data flow oriented specification techniques. Stresses the use of data flow diagrams and data dictionary.

Jackson, M.A., System Development, Prentice-Hall, 1983.

Still another approach to data structure oriented system design. Jackson offers many intriguing insights into the construction of software-based systems.

Martin, C.F., User-Centered Requirements Analysis, Prentice-Hall, 1988.

An interesting treatment of analysis that suggests methods for drawing the user into the process. Written with a definite IS focus, the book covers both functional and data analysis.

Δ **McMenamin, S., and J. Palmer, Essential Systems Analysis, Yourdon Press, 1984.**

This book introduces an important refinement of the logical and physical modeling approach proposed by most system analysis texts. Called the Essence-Implementation Model, this approach does much to clarify the amount of detail required to describe systems.

Mittra, S.S., Structured Techniques of System Analysis, Design and Implementation, Wiley-Interscience, 1988.

Design primarily for a data processing/IS audience, this book emphasizes front-end activities. Contains a good discussion of feasibility analysis. Good case studies.

Orr, K., Structured Requirements Definition, Ken Orr & Associates, Topeka, KS, 1981.

A description of the Warnier-Orr technique of data structure oriented specification. Introduces the notation and concepts that form the foundation of Data Structured Systems Development (DSSD).

Page-Jones, M., The Practical Guide to Structured Systems Design, Yourdon Press, 1980.

Another treatment of data flow oriented techniques. Jones provides additional insight.

Perkinson, R.C., Data Analysis: The Key to Data Base Design, QED, Wellesley, MA, 1984.

A worthwhile treatment of data analysis and design. Includes discussions of normalization, data base design, data requirements analysis and various data base architectures.

Ross, R.G., Entity Modeling: Techniques and Applications, Data Research

Group, Inc., Boston, 1988.

One of the few books written about E-R modeling, this short text presents an excellent overview of the subject. E-R techniques are presented with many examples and the use of CASE tools is considered.

Warnier, J.D., Logical Construction of Systems, Van Nostrand-Reinhold, 1981.

A discussion of data structure oriented specification by one of the founding fathers.

Δ **Yourdon, Edward, Modern Structured Analysis, Prentice-Hall, 1989.**

A comprehensive treatment of structured analysis by one of the "fathers" of the technique. Yourdon revisits, and in many cases, updates earlier concepts. Excellent discussion of both techniques and tools.

Δ **Yourdon, E. and Coad, P., Object-Oriented Analysis, Yourdon Press, 1990.**

The first attempt at coupling structured analysis and design with the underlying concepts of OO. Introduces a new notation and extends existing concepts.

Formal Methods

Dijkstra, E., The Formal Development of Programs and Proofs, Addison-Wesley, 1989.

An advanced treatment of the subject, Dijkstra is one of the true innovators in computer science.

Dromey, R.G., Program Derivation, Prentice-Hall, 1989.

A detailed presentation of the mathematics of formal specification, this book establishes the necessary groundwork and then provides useful examples to illustrate the approach.

Tanik, M.M., Fundamentals of Computing for Software Engineers, VanNostrand Reinhold, 1991.

This book presents the mathematics and theory associated with formalism in software engineering. An worthwhile guide for those with little background in the subject.

Woodcock, J. and M. Loomis, Software Engineering Mathematics, Addison-Wesley, 1988.

An good introduction to formal systems, propositional and predicate calculus, set theory and other topics that are relevant to formal specification techniques.

Software Design —Conventional Methods

Cameron, J., JSP&JSD: The Jackson Approach to Software Development, IEEE Computer Society Press, 1989.

The most comprehensive treatment of the Jackson methodology published to date. This book combines original writing and reprinted papers to cover both the analysis and design components of the approach.Useful examples are presented.

Hansen, K., Data Structured Program Design, Ken Orr Associates, Topeka, KS, 1984.

A simplified description of Orr's Data Structured System Development (DSSD) method for software design.

Jones, C., Software Development: A Rigorous Approach, Prentice-Hall, 1980.

As its name implies, this book is intended for a more academic audience than most in this bibliography. However, it will be of interest to those with a computer science background.

King, M.J., and J.P. Pardoe, Program Design Using JSP, Halsted, 1985.

An excellent summary of the Jackson Structured Programming (JSP) approach. A worthwhile companion volume to Jackson's excellent book, System Development.

Δ Linger, R., H. Mills, and B. Witt, Structured Programming, Addison-Wesley, 1979.

The definitive treatment of structured programming as a procedural design tool. Excellent use of PDL and detailed discussion of design correctness proofs.

Marca, D.A., and C.L. McGowan, SADT, McGraw-Hill, 1988.

The most thorough treatment of SADT published to date, this book presents excellent coverage of this important analysis and design technique. Detailed discussion of SADT diagramming and examples from many different industry applications make this a worthwhile addition to the software engineering literature.

Martin, J., and C. McClure, Diagramming Techniques for Analysts and Programmers, Prentice-Hall, 1985. Δ

Probably the most comprehensive survey of analysis and design notation produced to date. Topics include structure charts, HIPO, Warnier-Orr, N-S diagrams, flowcharts, state transition diagrams, PDL, decision trees/tables, Jackson diagrams and many others.

Peters, L., Software Design: Methods and Techniques, Yourdon Press, 1981.

An overview of major design techniques, representation methods and procedural approaches. Contains source material on a number of obscure methods.

Warnier, J.D., Logical Construction of Programs, VanNostrand-Reinhold, 1976.

Describes an important data structure oriented design approach. Warnier takes a formal view, focusing on the hierarchy of information as the guiding criteria for good design.

Yourdon, E., and L. Constantine, Structured Design, Prentice-Hall, 1979. Δ

The seminal textbook describing data flow oriented design techniques. Detailed discussion of transform and transaction analysis, functional independence and other design issues.

Software Design—User Interfaces

Dumas, J.S., Designing User Interfaces for Software, Prentice-Hall, 1988.

A good introduction for user interface design. Provides worthwhile guidelines for data entry, information display and user-machine interaction.

Monk, A. (ed.), Fundamentals of Human Computer Interaction, Academic Press, 1984.

Contains invited chapters on many important aspects of human-machine interface design. Combines human psychological research with technical issues of machine interaction.

Rubin, T., User Interface Design for Computer Systems, Wiley, 1988.

Particularly useful for its discussion of "help" techniques, the use of color, and guidelines for evaluating user interface designs, this book is a worthwhile addition to every software engineering library.

Δ Shneiderman, B., Designing the User Interface, Addison-Wesley, 1987.

A thorough treatment of human-machine interface design by one of the experts in the field. Covers basic concepts and presents many guidelines for user interface design.

Software Design—Object-Oriented Methods

Δ   **Booch, G., Software Engineering with Ada, second edition, Benjamin-Cummings, 1987.**

A useful treatment of object-oriented techniques applied in the context of Ada. Includes a set of worthwhile examples. Also an excellent introductory text on the programming language Ada.

Booch, G., Software Components with Ada, Benjamin-Cummings, 1987.

An extension and refinement of his earlier book, Booch refines his approach to object-oriented design using Ada, presenting new and improved examples and substantially broader insight. The author emphasizes software reusability and its accomplishment through the Ada programming environment.

Δ **Booch, G. Object-Oriented Design, Benjamin-Cummings, 1990.**

A detailed treatment of object-oriented design that introduces a comprehensive notation for design, guidelines for a design method and a number of excellent examples that illustrate the process.

Buhr, R.J.A., System Design with Ada, Prentice-Hall, 1984.

The design method presented in this book combines data flow and object-oriented approaches and then couples them with an Ada implementation.

Cox, B., Object-Oriented Programming, Addison-Wesley, 1986.

A detailed treatment of object-oriented design and programming using the Smalltalk/Objective-C point of view. Introduces important concepts such as inheritance, encapsulation and messages.

Khoshafian, S. and R. Abnous, Object-Orientation, Addison-Wesley, 1990.

A thorough introduction to object-oriented technologies. Covers languages, databases, and user interfaces , emphasizing C++ and Ada.

Δ   **Myer, B., Object-Oriented Software Construction, Prentice-Hall, second edition ,1990.**

The best treatment of object-oriented methods published to date, Myer's book presents basic object-oriented concepts and a detailed discussion of key features of object-oriented systems. The Eiffel programming language is used to illustrate key points.

Object-Oriented Design Handbook, EVB Software Engineering, Inc., Rockville, MD, 1985.

A pragmatic "how-to" treatment of object-oriented design. EVB has adopted the object-operation approach proposed by Booch and has established a systematic OOD methodology best suited to the Ada programming language.

Peterson, G.E., Tutorial: Object-Oriented Computing, two volumes, IEEE Computer Society, 1987.

Another excellent IEEE tutorial, these volumes are an anthology of important papers on object-oriented techniques with connecting text and explanation provided by Peterson. Basic concepts are presented in the first volume and followed with specific applications in the second volume.

Rumbaugh, J., *et al*, **Object-Oriented Modeling and Design, Prentice-Hall, 1991.**

Introduces a comprehensive notation and step-by-step approach for OOD. Contains an interesting and reasonably detailed discussion of how one might relate functional modeling (structured analysis) with object-oriented modeling.

Shlaer, S. and S.J. Mellor, Object-Oriented Systems Analysis, Yourdon Press (Prentice-Hall), 1988.

A discussion of object-oriented approaches to analysis as opposed to design. Although the treatment focuses primarily on data design and entity-relationship modeling, the book is a worthwhile addition for those who want all views of O-O techniques.

Winblad, A.L., et al, Object-Oriented Software, Addison-Wesley, 1990.

An useful introduction to object-oriented technologies for the uninitiated. Covers languages, databases, and user interfaces as well as an overview of methods for analysis and design.

Software Design—Fundamental Topics

The following books (annotated comments have been omitted) may be used to review fundamental topics that are associated with software design and coding.

Data Structures (Data Design)

Barker, R., Entity-Relationship Modeling, Addison-Wesley, 1990.

Bracket, M.H., Practical Data Design, Prentice-Hall, 1990.

Brathwaite, K.S., Analysis, Design and Implementation of Data Dictionaries, McGraw-Hill, 1988.

Date, C.J., An Introduction to Data Base Systems, 4th edition, Addison-Wesley, 1986.

Dutka, A.F. and H.H. Hanson, Fundamentals of Data Normalization, Addison-Wesley, 1989.

Gupta, R. and E. Horowitz (eds.), Object-Oriented Databases with Applications to CASE, Networks, and VLSI CAD, Prentice-Hall, 1991.

Horowitz, E., and S. Sahni, Fundamentals of Computer Algorithms, Computer Science Press, 1978.

Kruse, R.L., Data Structures and Program Design, Prentice-Hall, 1984.

Lewis, T.G., and M.Z. Smith, Applying Data Structures, Houghton-Mifflin, 1976.

Tenenbaum, A.M., and M.J. Augenstein, Data Structures Using Pascal, Prentice-Hall, 1981.

Weiderhold, G., Database Design, 2nd edition, McGraw-Hill, 1983.

Programming Languages

Ledgard, H., and M. Marcotty, The Programming Language Landscape, SRA, 1981.

Pratt, T.W., Programming Languages, 2nd edition, Prentice-Hall, 1984.

Martin, J. , Fourth Generation Languages: Principles, Representative Languages, two volumes, Prentice-Hall, 1985, 1986.

Software Design—Real-Time Systems

Allworth, S.T., Introduction to Real-Time Software Design, Springer-Verlag, 1981.

A monograph on real time design. Introduces the concept of a real-time virtual machine as a guide to the design process.

Cooling, J.E., Software Design for Real-Time Systems, VanNostrand Reinhold, 1991.

Another of many books that addresses issues in real-time software engineering. Emphasis is on languages and programming issues.

Foster, R., Real-Time Programming—Neglected Topics, Addison-Wesley, 1981.

A pragmatic treatment of "the problems you run into when you try to connect a computer to the real world." Covers interrupts, ports, speed matching and other important topics.

Glass, R., Real-Time Software, Prentice-Hall, 1983.

Covers a broad range of topics relating to real-time software. Methodologies for design, implementation and test of real-time software are considered.

Δ **Hatley, D.J., and I.A. Pirbhai, Strategies for Real-Time System Specification, Dover House, 1987.**

This book presents one of two important real-time analysis and specification techniques (the other is described in Ward and Mellor's volumes described below). Contains excellent industry examples and a reasonably thorough exposition of the technique.

Heath, W.S., Real-Time Software Techniques, VanNostrand Reinhold, 1991.

A compact guide for those who must develop real-time software for embedded microprocessor applications.

Leigh, A.W., Real-Time Software for Small Systems, Wiley (Sigma), 1988.

Because the focus of this system is small microprocessor-based systems, it should be of particular interest to those reader who develop embedded product software. Covers testing and maintenance issues as well as design. Examples are worthwhile.

Levi, S. and A.K. Agrawal, Real-Time System Design, McGraw-Hill, 1990.

One of the more rigorous treatments of the subject, this book takes an object-oriented view and introduces a mathematical perspective missing in other texts. Also contains a discussion of verification techniques for real-time systems.

Mellichamp, D.A. (ed.), Real-Time Computing, Van Nostrand-Reinhold, 1983.

A comprehensive treatment of all aspects of real-time systems including hardware, software and interfacing. Focus is on real-time process control and monitoring and software applications in a laboratory setting.

Siewiork, D.P., et al., Computer Structures, Principles and Examples, McGraw-Hill, 1982.

A voluminous treatment of all aspects of computer-based systems design. Although the book has a decided hardware orientation, it should be of interest to real-time system engineers.

Vick, C.R., and C.V. Ramamoorthy, Handbook of Software Engineering, Chapters 5-9, Van Nostrand-Reinhold, 1984.

These chapters focus on real-time computing issues and include treatments of real-time control, emulation, hardware-software trade-offs, systems issues and other topics. Contains an extensive bibliography on real-time software.

Δ **Ward, P.T., and S.J. Mellor, Structured Development for Real-Time Systems, 3 volumes, Yourdon Press, 1985, 1986.**

This three volume set presents a worthwhile notation and approach to real-time software design that is adapted from conventional data flow oriented methods. Vol. 1 introduces the subject, Vol. 2 presents analysis methods, and Vol. 3 discusses design approach. Highly recommended.

Software Quality Assurance and Testing

Δ **Beizer, B., Software System Testing and Quality Assurance, Van Nostrand-Reinhold, 1984.**

An excellent treatment of system/software testing strategies and their relationship to SQA. Beizer reproduces worthwhile material from his earlier book on software testing and then extends this with excellent material on system-related issues. Detailed information is presented on each test step.

Δ **Beizer, B., Software Testing Techniques, Van Nostrand-Reinhold, 1983.**

Comprehensive treatment of many important testing techniques. Detailed consideration of path testing and Boolean algebraic techniques.

Berg, H.K., et al., Formal Methods for Program Verification and Specification, Prentice-Hall, 1982.

For those readers with a theoretical bent, this text presents a detailed treatment of formal verification models for software.

Cho, C.K, Quality Programming, Wiley, 1987.

A rigorous treatment of the techniques for developing and testing software with statistical quality control, this book is an important addition to the quality assurance literature. Cho presents a remarkably readable mix of pragmatic guidelines and statistical theory. Discussions of both SQA and testing techniques are presented.

Dunn, R., Software Defect Removal, McGraw-Hill, 1984.

Presents methods for static and dynamic testing. Also considers other SQA elements.

Dunn, R., Software Quality Assurance, Prentice-Hall, 1990.

An introduction to SQA with an emphasis on pragmatic management issues. Considers SQA planning and the tasks associated with the activity.

Dunn, R., and R. Ullman, Quality Assurance for Computer Software, McGraw-Hill, 1982.

One of the few books that present a practical treatment of the procedures and techniques required to institute SQA in an organization.

Evans, M.W., Productive Software Test Management, Wiley, 1984.

One of the few books dedicated to the management issues associated with testing. Presents detailed discussions of test planning, control, scheduling and other management topics.

Evans, M.W., and J.J. Marciniak, Software Quality Assurance and Management, Wiley, 1986.

A management oriented view that contains good information on software quality evaluation, metrics, product issues and data control. Makes use of the latest IEEE SQA standards.

Δ **Freedman, D., and G. Weinberg, Handbook of Walkthroughs, Inspections and Technical Reviews, 3rd edition, Dorset House, 1990.**

Written in an unusual question and answer format, this book presents a complete introduction to reviews as a quality assurance mechanism for computer software. A wide variety of useful checklists, forms and guidelines is presented.

Hetzel, W., The Complete Guide to Software Testing, QED, 1984.

An introductory survey of all important aspects of testing. Although somewhat superficial, the text presents a useful discussion of testing at each step in the software engineering process.

Hollecker, C.P. Software Reviews and Audits Handbook, Wiley, 1990.

Contains detailed step-by-step guidelines for conducting formal technical reviews and audits.

Howden, W.E., Functional Program Testing and Analysis, McGraw-Hill, 1987.

One of the more mathematical of all testing books, Howden's treatment of the subject considers both practical and theoretical issues. Heavy emphasis on function definition and verification distinguishes this book from others.

McCabe, T., Structured Testing, IEEE Computer Society, 1982.

A detailed treatment of McCabe's Basis Path Testing technique. Includes discussion of software complexity and its use in test case design.

Δ **Musa, J.D., A. Iannino, and K. Okumoto, Software Reliability, McGraw-Hill, 1987.**

This book is the most thorough treatment of software reliability published to date. A rigorous treatment of the subject, the book also contains an excellent introduction, worthwhile practical examples and a copious discussion of theory.

Δ **Myers, G., The Art of Software Testing, Wiley, 1979.**

Still the most widely referenced and quoted book on software testing. Introduces the reader to a variety of black-box and white-box testing techniques.

Perry, W.E., How to Test Software Packages, Wiley, 1986.

Worthwhile because it focuses on how to test software that has been delivered from another source within your company or purchased from the outside, this book describes useful methods for test planning and execution.

Δ **Schulmeyer, C.G. and J.I. McManus (eds.), Handbook of Software Quality Assurance, Van Nostrand, 1987.**

An excellent anthology of contributed chapters on SQA. Topics include QA management, SQA planning and organization, costs, personnel issues, reviews, software configuration management and much more. A worthwhile addition to every software engineering library.

Yourdon, E., Structured Walkthroughs, fourth edition, Yourdon Press, 1989.

A brief, but worthwhile, discussion of formal technical reviews. Concentrates on mechanics, psychology and management of walkthroughs.

Software Maintenance

Arthur, L.J., Software Evolution, Wiley-Interscience, 1988.

One of the more detailed (but still somewhat superficial) discussions of software maintenance, Arthur's book presents worthwhile discussions of "change management, impact analysis and re-engineering.

Martin, J. and C. McClure, Software Maintenance, Prentice-Hall, 1983.

This book is representative of most that are dedicated to software maintenance. Topics include methods for achieving "maintainability," maintenance procedures, new methodologies that may ease the maintenance burden and other topics.

Parikh, G., Handbook of Software Maintenance, Wiley, 1986.

A collection of useful guidelines for maintenance practitioners and managers who must control the process. Presents a useful discussion of how design methods can be applied during maintenance activities.

Zvegintzov, N and G. Parikh, Software Maintenance, IEEE Computer Society, 1983.

This anthology presents many important papers dedicated to software maintenance. Both management and technical topics are presented.

CASE, Tools, Environments, and Other Topics

Barstow, D.R., et al., Interactive Programming Environments, McGraw-Hill, 1984.

A collection of contributed papers and chapters that describe research efforts in "computer aided software engineering." Important information for builders of software tools.

Bennett, K.H., Software Engineering Environments, Halsted (Wiley), 1989.

A survey of recent research in software engineering environments. Written in the U.K., this book focuses primarily on European work in environments.

CASE Industry Directory, Case Consulting Group, Portland, Oregon, 1988.

Currently, the most comprehensive survey of existing CASE tools and vendors. An excellent source book for those who are investigating CASE tools.

CASE: The Potential and the Pitfalls, QED Information Sciences, Inc., Wellesley, MA, 1989.

The best textbook treatment of CASE published to date. Covers the technology, the tools and environments. Also included worthwhile case studies from a number of U.S. companies.

Charette, R.N., Software Engineering Environments, McGraw-Hill, 1986.

This book presents a detailed treatment of programming environments and associated software tools.

Fisher, A.S., CASE—Using Software Development Tools, Wiley, 1988.

Few books on CASE have been written to date and all have some weaknesses. However, this is currently the best available treatment of the subject. Topics include basic principles, environments, descriptions of current tools.

Kernighan, B.W., and P.J. Plauger, Software Tools in Pascal, Addison-Wesley, 1981.

A pragmatic discussion of generic algorithms (the authors call these "tools") for software development. An earlier version of this book focused on RATFOR (a Fortran dialect).

McClure, C., CASE is Software Automation, Prentice-Hall, 1988.

Although flawed in many ways, this book presents an early attempt at describing computer aided software engineering. Worthwhile introduction to some aspects of CASE for the beginner but narrow in scope and content.

Spurr, K. and P. Layzell (eds.), CASE on Trial, Wiley, 1990.

The primary lure of this book is the description of user experiences with CASE technology. Also contains useful discussion on selection and justification of tools.

Towner, L.E., CASE: Concepts and Implementation, McGraw-Hill, 1989.

Presents a useful overview of key issues in CASE—tools, environments and associated methods.

SOFTWARE ENGINEERING: OTHER INFORMATION SOURCES

Periodicals—Technical Content
   IEEE Transactions on Software Engineering
   Δ **Computer (IEEE Computer Society)**
   Δ **IEEE Software (IEEE Computer Society)**
   Communications of the ACM
   Δ **ACM Software Engineering (SIGSOFT) Notes**
   IEEE Software Engineering Technical Committee Newsletter

Newsletters—CASE
   Δ **CASE Outlook**
      (CASE Consulting Group, Lake Oswego, OR, quarterly, fax: 503-245-6935)
   Δ **CASE Strategies**
      (Cutter Information Corp., Arlington, MA, monthly, fax: 508-544-3779)
   CASE Trends
      (Software Productivity Group, Shrewsbury, MA, monthly, fax: 508-842-7119)
   CASE User
      (CASE Consulting Group, Lake Oswego, OR, monthly, fax: 503-245-6935)
   Executive Briefing: CASE
      (Context Publishing. Portland, OR, bi-monthly, fax: 503-232-8057)
Each of the newsletter companies also publishes reports on specific tools and other CASE topics.

Directories—CASE
   CASEBASE , an on-line database
      (P-Cube Corp., Brea, CA, 714-990-3169)
   CASE Locator, an on-line datadase
      (CASE Associates, Oregon City, OR, 503-656-3207)
   CASE Tools Directory
      (CASE Consulting Group, Lake Oswego, OR, fax: 503-245-6935)
   Testing Tools Reference Guide
      (Software Quality Engineering, Jacksonville FL, 904-268-8639)

Periodicals—General Content
   Δ **American Programmer (monthly)**
   Computerworld (weekly)
   Software News (monthly)
   Datamation (monthly)
   BYTE (monthly)

Conference Proceedings (held at regular intervals)
   Δ **International Conference on Software Engineering**
   COMPSAC, INFOCOM, SOFTCON
   Trends and Applications Conference
   Design Automation Conference

STANDARDS

Δ **Software Engineering Standards, third edition, IEEE, SH12534, 1989.**

   Over 500 pages long, this compendium of ANSI/IEEE standards for software engineering is absolutely essential for any software engineering library. Contains standards for Documentation, SQA, SCM, Testing, Reviews, Project Management, Requirements Specification, and Metrics.

APPENDIX II
SOFTWARE ENGINEERING TEACHING SYSTEM

The *Software Engineering Teaching System* includes the third edition of *Software Engineering: A Practitioner's Approach*, this *Instructor's Manual*, a collection of industry quality CASE tools, ten video-tape modules that introduce important concepts in software engineering and CASE, workbooks to go along with the video tapes (if you decide to assign the tape outside the classroom), and a complete set of transparency masters to complement your lectures.

With the exception of this *Instructor's Manual*, all supplementary materials included as part of the *Software Engineering Teaching System* are available for use on the industry level. Their availability as part of package for university instructors has been negotiated to provide you with the best possible approach for teaching software Engineering.

GENERAL TERMS AND CONDITIONS

IMPORTANT, PLEASE READ CAREFULLY:

The elements of the *Software Engineering Teaching System* that are available to the industry—transparencies, video tape modules and CASE tools—are provided to you at a deep discount that is a small percentage of the cost of the element in the industry marketplace. For this reason, all instructors that request these elements of the *Software Engineering Teaching System* must agree to abide by the following terms and conditions:

1. The *Software Engineering Teaching System* is available only to and may be used by accredited colleges and universities in the United States during those school terms for which *Software Engineering: A Practitioner's Approach*, 3d edition, has been adopted for classroom use.

2. Only one copy of each element of the *Software Engineering Teaching System* may be ordered by a given institution, regardless of the number of times that *Software Engineering: A Practitioner's Approach*, 3d edition, has been adopted.

3. All orders for the *Software Engineering Teaching System* must be validated by the McGraw-Hill Book Company before they are sent to a vendor for fulfilment.

4. The *Software Engineering Teaching System* may be used only in conjunction with "for credit" courses offered as part of an institution's normal computing curriculum. The elements of the system (including transparencies, video modules and tools) may **not** be used for "short courses," or for outside consulting activities performed by professors.

5. All *Software Engineering Teaching System* materials are protected by copyright and the institution agrees that no copies of materials will be made in either paper or magnetic form. The institution further agrees to take necessary steps to prevent students from illicitly copying any *Software Engineering Teaching System* materials.

6. Title to and ownership of all *Software Engineering Teaching System* materials shall remain with each of the vendors that holds copyright to the materials.

7. A copy of the book order requisition form from your school for the Pressman text.

NOTICE: The materials included as part of the *Software Engineering Teaching System* are made available through the generosity of participating companies and are provided as a service to you. Each company has agreed to make its best effort to deliver *Software Engineering Teaching System* materials to university and college instructors who agree to the above terms and conditions and who submit the fees required. However, availability is not guaranteed.

DISCLAIMER: The individual vendors, McGraw-Hill Book Company, and the author, make no warrantee, either express or implied, about the availability, fitness for a particular purpose or use of these materials. When available, they are provided "as is" without warrantee of any kind.

The individual vendors, McGraw-Hill Book Company, and the author reserve the right to discontinue offering any element of the *Software Engineering Teaching System* at any time without written notice.

A BRIEF DESCRIPTION OF THE ELEMENTS

TRANSPARENCY MASTERS

Over 200 hundred transparency masters are provided to complement your lectures. They are organized on a chapter-by chapter basis and have been designed both to emphasize important topics presented in each SEPA chapter and (in some cases) to introduce additional topics for discussion.

VIDEO MODULES

The video portion of the *Software Engineering Teaching System* is entitled "Understanding CASE" and has been developed in conjunction with Digital Equipment Corporation. The series is a set of 10 video modules and workbooks organized in three parts:

Part I—Management Issues and Strategies
Module 1.   Challenges of Software Development
Module 2.   CASE: A Technology Overview
Module 3.   Making Software Engineering Happen

Part II—Software Quality and Configuration Management
Module 4.   Software Configuration Management
Module 5.   Software Quality Assurance
Module 6.   Software Testing
Module 7.   Software Maintenance and CASE

Part III—Analysis, Design and CASE Technical Issues
Module 8.   Software Requirements Analysis and Specification
Module 9.   Software Design
Module 10. CASE: Technical Issues

Each video module is approximately one hour in length and is supplemented with a workbook that contains figures, further points of discussion and suggested references.

CASE TOOLS

The following the CASE tools available as part of the *Software Engineering Teaching System.*

Tool	Type	Hardware
EasyCASE Plus	Analysis & Design	IBM PC
MacBubbles	Analysis & Design	Apple Macintosh
smartCASE	Analysis & Design	IBM PC
SPQR/20	Project Management	IBM PC
TurboCASE	Analysis & Design	Apple Macintosh

The discounted cost of each of these tools is noted on the order form at the end of this appendix. To take advantage of the *Software Engineering Teaching System* price, **you must first obtain a validation card from McGraw-Hill** by returning the order form at the end of this appendix.

The pages that follow contain reproductions of vendor literature that provide a brief description of the features of each tool. Please be certain that your hardware is compatible with the tool before ordering.

Note: You may select only one of the four analysis and design tools that are offered. Please check **only one** tool from the analysis and design category on the order form.

Evergreen CASE Tools, Inc
EasyCASE Plus Version 3.0 $495

EasyCASE Plus is an easy to learn, easy to use, highly functional and affordable CASE diagramming tool which, together with an integrated data dictionary and several utilities, is designed to support the structured design and data and information modelling phases (known as "upper CASE") of the system software development life cycle. Multiple diagramming types are supported, including: data flow diagrams (DFDs); transformation schema; state transition diagrams; structure charts; entity relationship diagrams (ERDs); data model diagrams; and data structure diagrams. Multiple methodologies are supported, including Yourdon-DeMarco; Gane & Sarson; Yourdon-Constantine; Ward-Mellor; Chen, Bachman and Martin.

For chart drawing and editing, EasyCASE Plus provides many powerful features. Its IBM SAA/CUA compliant graphical user interface (GUI) includes mouse support, pull-down menus, shortcut keys, pop-up dialog boxes, icons, scroll bars, and a 'click and drag' approach to diagram object selection and manipulation making it very easy to learn and use. The user interface and menus are logically organized and are consistent across the various chart types. You can take advantage of user definable color for all aspects of the user interface including menus, dialog boxes, text, chart objects, error indications, object explosions etc. A drawing grid allows for easy placement and relocation of objects. A large drawing area is supported by several zoom, panning and scrolling methods. You can move chart objects, or the entire chart, around on the drawing surface by selecting and dragging to a new position. Connections and labels remain attached to chart objects even if moved, and automatic flow routing inserts line segments to smooth out diagonal connections. Group selection and manipulation of chart objects is supported, including group deletion, copying and move. You can save chart fragments to a disk file. Saved charts can be loaded or merged.

User selectable options are available to control the appearance of the chart, including a title block, grid display and colors. Also provided is the ability to choose open/closed/filled arrowheads, number of arrowheads, object size, symbol set, directed connections, rounded corners, line style etc. for flows and connections.

EasyCASE Plus features an integrated data dictionary, implemented directly in dBASE format. Chart objects, charts, text files, data structure definitions (records) and element definitions are stored as data dictionary entries.

Through the data dictionary you can name, label and attach attributes to chart objects and reuse objects or relate them to other objects. The data dictionary and object lists can be accessed from the chart using list boxes and populated using data entry screens. You can attach a textual description, definition and an alias to an object. You can define composite data structures and control tables using the Yourdon-DeMarco or Backus-Naur forms (=,+,(),{},[ ],** etc.). Several user definable object attribute fields are also available. You can link chart objects to other charts, text files and record and element definitions.

Chart linking enables you to link charts (same or different chart types) and the objects on them into hierarchical project diagram structures, via the data dictionary, allowing for top-down functional decomposition and partitioning of processes and flows. You can link chart objects such as data stores, flows, entities and relationships to common composite structure definitions. You can link control flows and stores to control tables. You can link data processes, modules, entities, etc. to text files for use as notes, process specifications, structure definitions, pseudocode or even source code and access them using the text editor provided or your own text editor or word processor. You can define database tables using record and element definitions.

The integrated data dictionary manager (DDM) allows for the addition of new objects and the browsing, deletion, un-deletion, modification, copying and renaming of existing objects defined in the data dictionary. The dictionary can be populated with object and definitions either via the chart editor, the DDM or an external DBMS such as dBASE III. you can also pack, sort, export, import and merge data dictionaries from other users or from other projects.

Some of the convenience features of EasyCASE Plus include: access to the data dictionary manager (DDM), reports manager, text editor and analysis capabilities, access to DOS and utility programs (including your word processor, DBMS, spreadsheet etc.) without leaving the chart editor; automatic chart file backup and export.

The EasyCASE Plus reports manager lets you print chart and data dictionary entry reports in full or summary to a printer, to the screen, or to a file. Several pre-defined reports allow checking of chart and data dictionary data.

EasyCASE Plus supports a wide variety of printers and plotters which are compatible with: Epson FX, Epson LQ, IBM Graphics, IBM Proprinter X24, HP QuietJet, PostScript, HP DeskJet or LaserJet at up to 300 dpi. Both letter (8.5" by 11") and 11" by 17" size paper are supported in portrait or landscape orientation. You can print an entire chart or select a specific portion. EasyCASE Plus can also print charts to a file in overwrite or append modes. In addition, EasyCASE Plus plots to HP 7475A, HP 7550A and 'generic' HPGL plotters. It can also plot charts to a file for use as a graphics metafile (HPGL) for import into word processors, etc. Scaling of charts is available when printing to PostScript printers or to HP Plotters.

Charts can be exported in PC Paintbrush, Windows Paint, HPGL and CGM (optional) file formats for import into word processor desktop publishing programs such as PageMaker, Ventura, WordPerfect etc. Chart object relationships and the data dictionary information can also be exported in dBASE III Plus and SDF formats for extended analysis, data entry, custom report generation, etc. Data dictionary information can be imported in dBASE III Plus and SDF formats.

An optional Level Balancing and Chart Verification add-on module (the analysis manager) enables you to check charts against a set of methodology and layout rules for object identification, definition and associations. Verify the consistency of ('level balance') processes, stores and flows on sets of related DFDs. Print chart verification and level balancing reports to printer, screen or file.

Requires DOS 3.0 or later, 640k memory (500k free), hard disk with 2MB free space, graphics adapter (EGA or VGA) and a Microsoft or compatible mouse. 80286 CPU recommended with 1MB expanded memory (EMS). Math coprocessor optional. Version 3.0. Comes with both 5.25" (1.2MB) and 3.5" diskettes. $495

Limited 30 day guarantee (disk envelope must remain sealed). Weight 4.0 pounds.

MacBubbles®

MacBubbles, version 2.0, is a integrated multi-window CASE tool designed to provide full support for structured analysis and design on the Apple Macintosh. This easy to learn, easy to use tool creates high quality data flow diagrams (DFDs), entity relationship diagrams (ERDs), state transition diagrams (STDs), and program structure charts (PSCs) using the full capabilities of the Apple LaserWriter. Only **MacBubbles** uses PostScript to provide curved data flows whose titles follow the shape of the data flow for easy identification. A data dictionary and mini-spec editor are included. The real-time DFD symbols of Boeing/Hatley, Ward & Mellor, and ESML are all supported.

Macbubbles supports the concepts of Essential Systems Analysis with custom functions that allow DFDs to be combined or leveled with a single click of the mouse. Expanded physical models containing hundreds of bubbles on a single diagram may be created when performing system archaeology. These large diagrams may be scaled to fit a single page or printed across multiple pages. Bubbles may be clicked open to reveal lower level diagrams or mini-specs. Data flows, data stores, entities and relationships may be clicked open to inspect or revise their data dictionary entries. Balancing checks may be requested or ignored as you wish. A variety of where-used cross-reference reports may be created as needed.

MacBubbles is more than just a tool for creating the products of structured analysis. It is a tool for doing the job itself. Changes are tracked by time and person and may be highlighted on output if desired. A variety of notes may be attached to graphic objects and dictionary entries to record decisions, information sources, open issues and other facts of operational or historical interest to analysts and managers. Effort metrics may also be tracked by individual document.

MacBubbles' economical price allows a copy to be provided for every analyst, thus eliminating support staff bottlenecks.

MacBubbles will run on any Apple Macintosh with at least 1 Meg of memory and System 6.0.4 or later. A PostScript® capable printer is needed for output.

MacBubbles was developed and is sold by StarSys, Inc., 11113 Norlee Drive, Silver Spring, MD 20902. The price of a single copy is $779.99. Quantity discounts begin with the second copy. A working demo version can be purchased for $25. An educator's copy will be provided to qualified colleges and universities for a shipping fee of $20 in North America and $40 elsewhere. A laboratory site license for student use is $200. Individual student versions may be purchased for $25 each.

smartCASE ™

The intelligent first step into CASE technology.

smartCASE is the newest addition to CADWARE's SYLVA family of CASE products. smartCASE is a PC-based diagramming and documentation tool for automation of CASE techniques and methods. smartCASE provides an economical and easy-to-use alternative to expensive CASE technology.

smartCASE can help with all your projects - from simple flow and organization charts to complex, rule-based, structured system designs.

smartCASE makes it easy to overcome the hurdle of bringing CASE methods and practices to your organization and provides the first step on the path to faster, more effective, more accurate system design and analysis.

And, smartCASE is upwardly compatible with CADWARE's team-level CASE products - System Developer I and System Developer II. So as your system development requirements increase, you can harness the the full power of CADWARE's proven CASE technology without reentering your information or retraining your staff.

Learn Industry Standards

smartCASE supports structured methods, information methods, and object-oriented methods, as well as complete flow and organization charting techniques. **smartCASE**'s interactive rule checking and context-sensitive, on-line HELP reduce errors and also provide cost-effective training for novice CASE users. With **smartCASE**, you not only create diagrams and charts, you also learn the principles of industry-standard CASE techniques.

Easy To Use

The **smartCASE** Diagram Editor uses an intuitive, icon-driven interface that is easy to learn, use, and remember. Creating diagrams is as simple as pointing and placing objects. Novice users can quickly begin creating designs and diagrams, and experienced users can concentrate on their projects and not on the tool. With **smartCASE**, you can benefit immediately from industry-proven CASE technology.

Open Architecture

smartCASE supports interfaces to popular word processors, making it easy to link your diagrams and charts to text documents. You can access up to four different word processing applications for mini-specifications, notes, pseudo-code, and other textual requirements.

smartCASE automatically links different diagrams in a hierarchical structure. There is no limit to the number of levels or the number of objects in one level. Child diagrams may use the same technique as the parent diagram or the user may choose to decompose in a different diagramming technique.

smartCASE also supports PostScript™ or Hewlett-Packard Graphics Language (HPGL)™ output, so you can use popular desktop publishing packages to produce quality documentation that increases the effectiveness and completeness of your projects.

CADWARE

BENEFITS

Proven structured techniques improve quality, maintainability of systems

Cost-effective way to utilize the latest CASE productivity tools

Errors are caught early in the life cycle thereby reducing the overall project cost

Inexpensive, easy-to-learn, easy-to-use CASE learning aid overcomes CASE cultural barriers in your organization

Increases project communication by using industry-standard techniques and methods to describe systems

CADWARE's SYLVA product line compatibility keeps training costs low as new tools are added

Automates most popular methods for analysis and design including structured, object-oriented, and information engineering planning and implementation

---

For more information, call

1-800-CADWARE

or contact us at:

CADWARE, Inc.
50 Fitch Street
New Haven, CT 06515

(203) 397-2908
FAX: (203) 387-0114

FEATURES

Eleven ICON DRUMS™ provide the following techniques, ranging from simple, free-form to rule-based, structured techniques:

> *Flow Chart*
> *Organization Chart*
> *Documentation*
> *DeMarco Data Flow*
> *Gane & Sarson Data Flow*
> *Ward-Mellor Control Flow*
> *Shlaer-Mellor Entity*
>   *Relationship Attribute*
> *Entity Relationship*
> *State Transition*
> *Constantine Structure*
> *Project Hierarchy*

On-line, context-sensitive help

Ability to create parent/child relationships between objects in different diagrams created with different methods

Every object in each diagram may have multiple references including four text files and a decomposition diagram

Access popular text editors/word processors and DOS without leaving Diagram Editor

HP Laser™, Epson™, or PostScript output directly to desktop publishing

Icon-based, point-and-place Diagram Editor interface

Editing functions include move, copy, zoom, cut/paste, size up/down

Automatic up/down level for hierarchical sets of diagrams

Automatic interactive and global rule checking

SYSTEM REQUIREMENTS

IBM PC/XT, PC/AT, PS/2, or 100% compatibles

640K conventional RAM memory

MS-DOS or OS/2

Monochrome or color monitor

EGA, VGA (EGA mode), CGA, or Hercules Monochrome graphics card

Hard Disk with 2MB free

1.2 or 1.44MB floppy disk drive (for installation)

About CADWARE...

CADWARE offers a unique combination of software products and services that help you with the development of complex systems. Our tools enable you to adapt your structured and object-oriented systems engineering environment to keep pace with ever-changing business and technical requirements.

CADWARE Sylva product line includes smartCASE, System Developer I, System Developer II, and Foundry.

CADWARE services include, training, hot line and maintenance support, and upgrade policies.

Unconditional 30 Day Money Back Guarantee

If you are not satisfied with **smartCASE** for any reason, return the entire package including documentation within 30 days, and we will issue you a full refund.

SPQR/20™ Estimator

The automated tool for planning and managing software development and maintenance projects

The new generation of software project managers is benefiting from a new kind of automated project estimator. It answers such "unanswerable" questions as

- How long will the project take?
- How much will it cost?
- How many people will it take?

And resolves critical technical issues such as

- How many function points will be included?
- How much code will be needed?
- What tools and methods will be most effective?
- Will it meet our users' needs?
- Will the quality be good enough to get the job done?

Early users of these estimating tools have enthusiastically embraced SPQR/20 as the most reliable, most detailed, and most convenient software project estimator.

The key elements forecast by SPQR/20 are captured in its name: Software Productivity, Quality, Reliability. (The number 20 refers to the number of variables included in the estimating model.)

HOW IT WORKS

SPQR/20 runs on an IBM PC or compatible computer. It prompts you through a series of easy-to-use screens and asks you to enter data about the planned software project:

- Type of project -- is it a new program, an enhancement, or a maintenance effort?

- Project estimating goals -- what staff size will be required; what are the possible tradeoffs?

- Information about the program code: language(s) used, reusability of existing code, etc.

- Type of program (i.e, batch application, interactive data base, real time or embedded, etc.)

- Environmental factors (staff experience, program design, code reusability, etc.)

SPQR uses this data to generate an estimate of a given software engineering scenario. It can also perform immediate, comparative estimates from new data inputs.

ABOUT SPQR'S OUTPUT

Your SPQR forecast provides key information about each alternative development plan. You can use this data to make key decisions about how to proceed with the project. Once the project is under way, the data can be reentered to manage the implementation and maintenance of the software system.

```
                SPQR SCHEDULE, EFFORT, STAFF, AND COST ESTIMATES

SECURITY - COMPANY CONFIDENTIAL          PROJECT:  RESOURCE PLANNING
                                         MODE 1 :  HIGHEST QUALITY

ACTIVITY                SCHEDULE      EFFORT      STAFFING        COSTS
                        (MONTHS)      (MONTHS)

PLANNING                  1.22          1.22        1.00          6,104
REQUIREMENTS              2.25          7.17        3.19         35,831
DESIGN                    3.69         17.42        4.72         87,080
CODING                    3.88         34.02        8.77        170,095
INTEGRATION/TEST          2.99         26.68        8.93        133,381
DOCUMENTATION            3.58         13.07        3.65         65,326
MANAGEMENT               10.29         12.86        1.25         64,304

DEVELOPMENT              14.03        112.42       10.92        562,122
OVERLAPPED               10.29
UNPAID OVERTIME                        14.61

                        SPQR MAINTENANCE ESTIMATES

             ENHANCEMENTS   REPAIRS    TOTAL      STAFFING      COSTS
             (MONTHS)      (MONTHS)    (MONTHS)               (DOLLARS)

YEAR 1        13.77          2.80       16.58       1.38        82,895
YEAR 2        14.46          1.52       15.99       1.33        79,940
YEAR 3        15.19          0.85       16.03       1.34        80,169
YEAR 4        15.95          0.47       16.42       1.37        82,084
YEAR 5        16.74          0.24       16.99       1.42        84,941

MAINTENANCE   76.12          5.89       82.01       1.37       410,029

TOTAL PROJECT
                           EFFORT     STAFFING        COSTS

DEVELOPMENT                112.42      10.92          562,122
MAINTENANCE                82.01        1.37          410,029
OTHER COSTS                                                 0

TOTAL PROJECT             194.43      12.29          972,151

                    SPQR NORMALIZED OUTPUTS

                          SOURCE LINES PER       FUNCTION POINTS PER
                          UNIT: (MONTHS)         UNIT: (MONTHS)
WITHOUT REUSED CODE
EXCLUDING UNPAID OVERTIME

    ALL DEVELOPMENT            356                    3.12
    CODING ONLY              1,176                   10.32

INCLUDING UNPAID OVERTIME

    ALL DEVELOPMENT            310                    2.72
    CODING ONLY              1,022                    8.97
```

SPQR provides information such as:

- Productivity gains to be expected when using certain tools or methodologies

- Total source code and function points needed to develop the proposed program or system (in any of 30 commonly used programming languages)

- Normalized productivity data, as measured by source code per person-month, cost per source line, cost per function, and function points per person-month

- Effort and dollar costs for all key development activities

- Staffing required for all major activities

- Estimated schedules by activity, and suggestions for possible overlapping of activities to reduce total time spent

- Enhancement and maintenance costs for five years of production

- Quality and reliability of the program or system being developed

- Detailed risk analysis to warn of potential hazards

- Amount of documentation needed to support requirements, specifications, user documentation, on-line screens, etc.

- Handles foreign currency (Version 1.3)

CAPERS JONES AND PROGRAMMING PRODUCTIVITY

CAPERS JONES, designer of the SPQR line of estimators and other productivity tools, is founder and Chairman of Software Productivity Research, Inc. He is a leader in the field of programming productivity, internationally known as a consultant, seminar leader, lecturer and author. One of his IEEE publications, *Programming Productivity: Issues for the Eighties*, remains one of their ten all time best sellers. He is also author of *Programming Productivity* in McGraw Hill's Software Engineering Series.

Prior to forming SPR, Inc., Mr. Jones played key roles in software productivity at several major international corporations, including IBM and ITT. He has served as productivity consultant to more than 200 corporations.

FOR MORE INFORMATION

Call Software Productivity Research, Inc. or send in the mailer below, to learn how SPQR/20 can help you plan and manage your next software development or maintenance project. Be sure to ask about our SPQR demonstration disk.

SPR **Software Productivity Research, Inc.**
77 South Bedford Street
Burlington, MA 01803
(617) 273-0140

PLEASE TELL US MORE ABOUT THE SPQR/20 ESTIMATOR

Name	Title	
Company Name	Phone	
Street	Mail Stop	
City	State	Zip

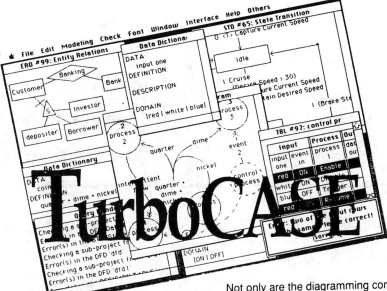

TurboCASE is a computer-aided software engineering vehicle that will speed you through the analysis stage of software development. Supporting multiple structured analysis methodologies and diagram styles, **TurboCASE** uses the power and ease of your Macintosh computer to make the learning fast too.

TurboCASE is a second generation CASE tool. StructSoft has also developed one of the top selling pc-based CASE tools, now being distributed as Teamwork/PCSA by Cadre Technologies, Inc. PCSA introduced some of the interface breakthroughs that have been refined and expanded in TurboCASE.

TurboCASE HANDLES LIKE A DREAM

TurboCASE does not rely simply on the Mac interface to claim "EASY TO USE." Consider this: the commands that you need for any operation are usually at the tip of your cursor—wherever your cursor may be! Not buried in sub menus requiring you to exercise your memory and practice "mousing navigation." And not somewhere across the screen in a toolbox. These commands are in object oriented pop-up menus, meaning that you get the right list of commands for the job you are about to do, simply by clicking where you want to do it.

Not only are the diagramming commands convenient and easy to find, but dictionary definitions and other parts of your specification are just a mouse click away, with Hypertext-like simplicity. And up to ten windows may be open at the same time on your screen, so you can always see the context for your next step.

TALK ABOUT POWER!

TurboCASE supports a wide range of methodologies for performing structured and real-time analysis:

✔ Yourdon/DeMarco—Structured Analysis
✔ Gane/Sarson — Structured Analysis
✔ McMenamin and Palmer—Essential Systems Analysis
✔ Chen—Entity relationship Modeling (data modeling)
✔ Hatley/Pirbhai—Real-time Modeling
✔ Ward/Mellor—Real-time modeling
✔ ESML—Real-time Modeling

Comprehensive Real-time Modeling: TurboCASE supports Extended System Modeling Language (ESML) which provides State Transition analysis, Decision Table analysis, and Process Activation analysis. All are suitable for Real-time Embedded System Modeling.ESML can model both the Ward/Mellor and the Hatley/Pirbhai methodologies.

Dig up your	Now try
"wish list" of	TurboCASE
things you know a	and see if it doesn't
CASE tool *should* do	surpass your greatest
for you...	expectations!

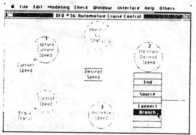

TurboCASE uses object oriented pop-up menus.

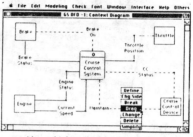

... provides multiple methodology support.

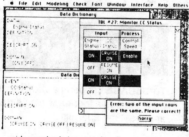

...with completely integrated on-line consistency checking.

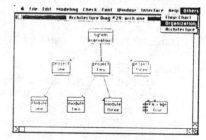

...and is built on a flexible architecture for adaptation to future methodologies & techniques.

Diagram Types:

TurboCASE supports a wide spectrum of diagram

styles and types, including **data flow** diagrams •

entity relationship diagrams • **structure charts** •

state transition diagrams • **mini-specifications** •

flow charts • and **organization charts**.

ABOVE AND BEYOND STANDARD FEATURES

✔ Supports splitting, merging and pruning of data flows and sub flows—with full consistency via the dictionary.
✔ Allows you to associate and disassociate diagrams freely.
✔ Assists you to insert levels, renumber, combine, or expand diagrams.
✔ Provides Requirements Traceability

WITH STATE OF THE ART ENGINEERING...

Analysis Techniques: TurboCASE represents a breakthrough for CASE technology by incorporating innovative automation for such techniques as Event Partitioning (or, abstracting a group of processes by "sending them up" as a single symbol to a new parent diagram) in a bottom-up approach to analysis.

Data Dictionary: Any information entered in one part of your project automatically becomes available to you when other aspects of the project are modeled. For instance, as you proceed from a data flow diagram to a decision table—or a state transition diagram—half the work is already done when you get there. Simply select from lists of possible inputs or transitions or processes (which are derived instantly from information on the parent diagram). You will never need to enter the same information twice. You simply select from a list of information that TurboCASE knows is appropriate for your next move, or you search for it.

Consistency Checks: TurboCASE keeps the consistency between diagrams current *at all times!* TurboCASE detects inconsistencies in the model and instantly sends you a message so that the problem can be fixed immediately.

In addition to balancing parent and child data flow diagrams, TurboCASE also balances state transition diagrams or decision tables with their corresponding data or control flow diagrams. Modifications at one level are updated on all levels—all the time.

TEAM PROJECT SUPPORT:

Diagrams, text files and the dictionary are transformed into an ASCII format for storage in external databases, configuration management, and for use with other CASE tools.

Large projects can be partitioned to allow parallel development by engineering teams. Each team member builds a small part of the overall system, then with TurboCASE's merge function, the pieces integrate into a single, complete project model.

SYSTEM SPECIFICATIONS:

TurboCASE is compatible with the entire Macintosh SE and II families.

The TurboCASE graphics architecture allows fast expansion to new graphics environments. If your need for a graphic language is unique or specialized please inquire for customization possiblities.

INFORMATION FOR ORDERING THE
SOFTWARE ENGINEERING TEACHING SYSTEM

1.   Decide which elements of the *Software Engineering Teaching System* you want to order.

2.   Be certain that your department Chairman or Dean has read and agrees to abide by the general terms and conditions (presented in this appendix) associated with the acquisition of the *Software Engineering Teaching System*.

3.   Complete the order form on the following page and mail it to the address at the bottom of the order form.

4.   If you are going to order CASE tools, you must first obtain a validation card from McGraw-Hill for each CASE tool that you have ordered. Send the validation card, along with a check to cover the fulfilment fee directly to the CASE vendor. The CASE tool will then be shipped directly to you.

ORDER FORM
SOFTWARE ENGINEERING TEACHING SYSTEM

Name: _____

Institution: _____

Department: _____

Address: _____

City, State, Zip: _____

Purchase Order No. (if necessary): _____

We have adopted *Software Engineering: A Practitioner's Approach*, 3d edition (SEPA). We would like to order one or more elements of the *Software Engineering Teaching System*. We have read the terms and conditions and the disclaimer contained in Appendix II of the Instructor's Manual for SEPA and agree to abide by them. I have attached a copy of the book order form for SEPA.

Signature: _____   Date: _____

ORDERING INFORMATION

Transparency Masters and Videos

The following Software Engineering Teaching System materials are available directly from McGraw-Hill.

_____   **transparency masters** (no charge, this request will be sent to your McGraw-Hill representative for processing) (ISBN 074545-5)

_____   **video modules and workbooks** ($395.00 fulfillment fee which will be billed to your address above) (ISBN 050819-4)

CASE Tools

(Do not send payment now. A validation card will be sent to you by McGraw-Hill. You will then send the card to the CASE vendor with your payment):

_____   SPQR/20 Estimator ($50.00 fulfillment fee)

Only one (1) of the following may be ordered:

_____   EasyCASE Plus (for the IBM PC or PS/2) ($50.00 fulfillment fee)

_____   MacBubbles (for the Apple Macintosh) ($20.00 fulfillment fee)

_____   smartCASE (for the IBM PC or PS/2) ($75.00 fulfillment fee)

_____   TurboCASE (for the Apple Macintosh) ($100.00 fulfillment fee)

Please send this form to: **Computer Science Marketing Manager, College Division, 43rd Floor, McGraw-Hill, Inc., 1221 Avenue of the Americas, New York, New York 10020.**

ORDER FORM
SOFTWARE ENGINEERING TEACHING SYSTEM

Name: _____

Institution: _____

Department: _____

Address: _____

City, State Zip: _____

Purchase Order No. (if necessary): _____

We have adopted *Software Engineering: A Practitioner's Approach*, 3d edition (SEPA). We would like to order one or more elements of the *Software Engineering Teaching System*. We have read the terms and conditions and the disclaimer contained in Appendix II of the *Instructor's Manual* for SEPA and agree to abide by them. I have attached a copy of the book order requisition form for SEPA.

Signature: _____ Date: _____

ORDERING INFORMATION

Transparency Masters and Videos

The following *Software Engineering Teaching System* materials are available directly from McGraw-Hill.

_____ **transparency masters** (no charge, this request will be sent to your McGraw-Hill representative for processing) (ISBN 074545-5)

_____ **video modules and workbooks** ($395.00 fulfilment fee which will be billed to your address above) (ISBN 050819-4)

CASE Tools

(Do not send payment now. A validation card will be sent to you by McGraw-Hill. You will then send the card to the CASE vendor with your payment):

_____ SPQR/20 Estimator ($50.00 fulfilment fee)
Only one (1) of the following may be ordered:
_____ EasyCASE Plus (for the IBM PC or PS/2)   ($50.00 fulfilment fee)
_____ MacBubbles (for the Apple Macintosh) ($20.00 fulfilment fee)
_____ smartCASE (for the IBM PC or PS/2) ($75.00 fulfilment fee)
_____ TurboCASE (for the Apple Macintosh) ($100.00 fulfilment fee)

Please send this form to: **Computer Science Marketing Manager, College Division, 43rd Floor, McGraw-Hill, Inc., 1221 Avenue of the Americas, New York, NY 10020.**